HOW TO TEXT A GIRL

A Complete Guide for Men To Approaching Women With Online Dating

Shane Farnsworth

due to the information herein, either directly or indirectly. The author owns all copyrights not held by the publisher.

The information herein is provided for educational purposes exclusively and is universal. The presentation of the data is without contractual agreement or any kind of warranty assurance.

All trademarks inside this book are for clarifying purposes only and are possessed by the owners themselves, not allied with this document.

Disclaimer

All erudition supplied in this book are specified for educational and academic purpose only. The author is not in any way in charge of any outcomes that emerge from using this book. Constructive efforts have been made to render information that is both precise and effective; however, the author is not to be held answerable for the accuracy or use/misuse of this information.

Foreword

I will like to thank you for taking the very first step of trusting me and deciding to purchase/read this life-transforming book. Thanks for investing your time and resources on this product.

I can assure you of precise outcomes if you will diligently follow the specific blueprint I lay bare in the information handbook you are now checking out. It has transformed lives, and I strongly believe it will equally transform your own life too.

All the information I provided in this Do It Yourself piece is easy to absorb and practice.

INTRODUCTION

This book is not about getting you more texts coming from girls. It's certainly not about that, because I do not assume that's what you yearn for. I don't assume you desire to be as bright as you can be in your texting. And I don't assume you would like to make her fall for your text messages.

I believe what you want is to be capable of getting her to say YES when you ask her out or ask her to meet up. That's precisely what this book is about.

The book is most likely to challenge a few of the most cherished conventional beliefs on "good texting." If a few of these challenges I toss your way make you a little uncomfortable, that's good. What I want you to accomplish when that takes place is to take the empiricist's perspective and say, "Okay, let me attempt it."

Your intuition might point out, "She would certainly never do that," but often, your intuition lies when it comes to trying something new.

The emphasis here is not to build your ego unnecessarily or fill your head with platitudes. Instead, the main objective of this book is to get her off the phone and on a date with you.

CHAPTER ONE

Your Objective in Texting

Let's begin with the fundamentals and strategy of texting ladies. This is what will effectively drive how you structure your messages and how you view texting generally.

Most text messages from men have a slipshod approach: they text girls without any definite aim. It is not sure just how they expect objective-free and direction least ext messages to achieve much.

This book will shine a little light on texting and get you in the right direction. You will ever have two objectives when texting, and they ought to never overlap. Here are the common objectives in texting ladies: (1) Build rapport and comfort, or (2) Set up a meet.

The number 2 (set up a meet) is your core objective. And the rapport-building or comfort-building you do in #1 must remain in operation to make to 2 a reality. Beyond that, these two objectives are the core.

It has been observed that a lot of men that text has a kind of pseudo-objective... like "keep texting her, then fish around in some way to get a date."This awful, atrocious quasi-objective leads men to send all sorts of half-baked text-- messages that leave a girl staring at her phone and asking herself, "Why the hell is he texting me this?" All these types of texts do is torpedo a guy's efforts towards getting the girls interest. Thumbs down for the pseudo-objective. If you are one of those who do that, stop it now.

When you send text, a woman should recognize right away what your objective is. And if you remember the two goals earlier referred to, they are: (1) build rapport and comfort, or (2) set up a meet. You want her to be capable of telling straightaway what the text is all about. The reason you wouldn't want any overlap is that as soon as you mix date demands with chit-chat, it becomes messy. That is when you see a guy fish around as he builds rapport, seeking for some way to transition into asking her out. Do not fall into this trap; Keep your objectives distinct. Either you text her intending to build rapport, or you text her to set up a meet.

Don't beat around the bush. Don't text without any objective. Don't send lots and whole lots of content. Don't get too wordy. Be straightforward and direct. Do text with your goal in mind. Do send a handful of strategic texts. Be concise and accurate. You should regularly be trying either to build rapport and comfort, or set up a meet.

Cold Texting and Warm Texting

It's essential to understand the distinction between cold and warm texting. When you text a girl that is thinking about you or even expecting to hear from you at the time you text her, that is warm texting. While cold texting is when you text a girl that is not in any way thinking about you or even expecting to hear from you when you text her,

Why the distinction? Given that you're going to adjust your tone to match exactly how prepared she is to talk to you, I'll give you examples:

First, envision, you're off to meet a male colleague for lunch. You're friendly with him but not very close. He sends you a text: "Just parked my car. Grab a table yet?" This may be the first text he's sent you all time, but it feels normal because you anticipated hearing from him.

Let's now imagine it's 10 am the next day, and you are busy with some work you don't like doing. You'd rather be back in bed. Then, you receive a text coming from that same coworker, which reads: "Just had my second cup of Joe. How's your morning?" To an exceptionally social individual, it could be trendy to receive this text ... however, most individuals will find this intrusive and strange. They will wonder, "Why did he text me? What does he want?"

That is the difference between cold and warm text messages. The first one-- where you considered to meet your coworker-- was normal, since you needed to know when and where to meet. The second one, though-- where would that originate from? This isn't a guy you're very close with. Is he making an effort to become buddies with you? Does he desire something from you? Does he have some form of a crush on you? Those are the type of confusing questions that would stand out in your head when a crisp text isn't structured right. Structure it inappropriately, and it can quickly appear like it just happened from nowhere.

Proper Ways to Structure Your Texts

The moment you send your first message in anew text conversation, there are a few elements you often would like to feature. For our purpose, a new text conversation (with a cold text) begins whenever the old conversation reaches a natural end. No exceptions, regardless of whether you only spoke to her via the phone. This is still a new conversation, even if you just changed channels.

The components to include in a new text conversation are: (a) Greeting, (b) Her name, (c) a new relevant information, and (d) something that presents consideration for her.

Each of these plays a major role in the "real feel" of the text. Below's what a complete first text along with all the features look like:

" Gabby, hello. Running a bit behind, sorry; it will certainly be there closer to 2:30. Still cool?"

We have:

(a) The greeting: "hey" (b) Her name: "Gabby."

(c) Some info: "Running a bit behind"-- "will be there closer to 2:30" (d) A little bit of consideration: "sorry"-- "Still cool?".

The fact that you texted to let her understand you will be late in the 1st place--that also counts as consideration.

In certain instances, we can quickly lose the greeting, and it still feels fine, mainly if the text is warm and comfortable. Therefore in the example above, we can drop the greeting (hey), and it is still fine because she expects you to deal with logistical issues in the run-up to the date. Often, though, you will wish to include the greeting-- it improves the possibility you'll get a positive response.

Next off, you should always use a girl's name in the first message of a new text conversation. This trips a mental trigger that assures her that you're speaking to her. Text, phone, and email don't just feel that person when you do not use the other person's name.

Exclamation points and emoticons have a lot more upside than downside. They'll add more benefits to your text and help compensate for the absence of body language, voice tone, etc.

If you make use of periods, your message will appear like this:

" Hey, Jim. I hope your week has been perfect. Seem like mine's never going to end."

If I get this type of message from a girl, It makes me think the girl's a downer; she appears whiny, and I get worried that if I meet her, she'll drag me into negative topics or even she'll get clingy and too dependent if we meet.

Surprisingly, some researchers have found out that people rate text that ends in periods, like the one cited above, as a lot less sincere than text messages without them.

Now, compare that earlier message to this:

" Hi, Jim! I hope your week has been perfect:) Feels like mine's never going to end..!".

Doesn't that feel fresher, energetic, and stunning! I can not wait to meet this girl. The same message, with different punctuation at the end of the sentences, She's likely to be a breath taken. Our text messages (as men) will not be that bouncy since we won't be texting just as ladies text, but it'll be related.

Texting is just one of those mediums from which you've to choose. In this instance, the choice is between masculine and negative or feminine and positive. I'll go for feminine and positive and count on my real life masculinity to plow under any kind of worries of my text being too adorable. Despite these features, texting still feels more natural than face-to-face communication. You can not much afford to do without them and go through a lot more unnatural feeling.

One more point to keep in mind on text messages is grammar. How grammatically correct should you be?

The challenge with regards to grammar is becoming loose enough to look informal, but positively not careless that you appear ignorant. Individually, what this means will vary by subculture, nation, continent, and age. I can't tell you precisely what syntax to use because it might be the wrong grammar for your age or where you reside! I will say this, though: your aim with grammar needs to be making your text persona match your in-person persona as much as you can.

Text works better as an extension of the person. Hence, if you've acquired an incredible office works and you suit up correctly and appear to be good, you won't wish to text her:

" Wat up bae, would u like to eat some food with me?"

Even though you're the local crack dealer, you yearn for cleaner grammar than this. Usually, a slang is more challenging to understand, and the more complicated your texts are to understand, the less she will go through and answer them. Don't forget, mental loads. Casualness as a stylistic choice is indeed excellent; going too far into way too much shorthand is all you should avoid as much as possible.

Thus far, we've talked about greetings, syntax, names, and punctuation. Next, we will discuss the other two elements to feature in every new text conversation: Information and Consideration.

The relevant information you discuss is the "point" of the text; it's the main reason why you texted. The consideration is the "bond" in the text; it's your duty to show consideration and care for this girl.

You should make true feelings when you text her because without that, you're weak. If she is baffled about why you sent the text or she thinks that it's cold, you aren't focusing much on her (lack of consideration), she'll have unpleasant feelings with regards to the text correspondence and be less likely to respond favorably.

The relevant information could be:

" Stuck here in this serious gridlock ... this town has the worst traffic!".

" Had the most delicious shrimp of my life last night ... I may still taste it.".

" Thinking we just have to get together soon.".

The consideration can be:

" How's your week looking like?".

" How was your test?"."

 What's your schedule for today?".

I also advise you use something like, "What's your full week looking like?" That's because I find it a fantastic, open-ended question to:

(a) get a girl to chat just about anything fun, different, or fascinating going on in her life, and

 (b) put together avenue for us to meet up.

Below's what our text to these girls should look like:

"Hi Lily, hope your weekend was great =) Sitting here in gridlock... this town has the worst traffic ever! How's your week looking?"

"Jane, Good morning! I had the most tasty shrimp of my life last night... I can still taste it. How did your test go?"

"Hey, Mary! Thinking we need to get together very soon. What's your schedule looking like this week?"

These are trendy, lovely, and personal, and will often get you the expected response. How she gets your messages is influenced partially by the preliminary perception you made on the girl you're sending out messages to, obviously, and also partially by precedent (for instance; if your first perception was bad for whatever reason, or if you've now set poor criterion in your correspondence where you text her, but she disregards your text, a first message now might be somehow too late), but usually, structured in this manner, you'll often get a response from women, and also they'll practically be at the very least slightly warm in their replies.

Ways to Text a Girl and Build Rapport.

It is recommended that you send an introductory text to a woman one to four hours after the initial meeting with her. If you met her towards the end of the night in a bar, at the nightclub, at a party, or on the street, one or two hours later is fine if you're practically heading to bed.

This introductory text is to break the communication ice systematically. The importance of this is that you want her to get comfortable interacting with you... but don't forget that you aren't attempting to know her this way.

The catch with communication comfort is: the longer you wait, the much more unpleasant the first contact will be (whether via a text or phone call). Send a text within one to four hours so as to protect against any awkwardness or anticipation settling in. This means you establish rapport via text message as soon as possible.

All you are expected to do to break the text ice is send a basic message like:

" Glad to come in contact with a fellow traveler -- -Frank."

or

"Delighted to meet someone like you tonight---Tommy."

So you give her:

(a) a goodwill statement to let her know you're glad you met her,

(b) a smiley face to share warmth and lovely feelings, and

(c) your name.

The above works as follows:

It helps build rapport. You've quickly moved to develop rapport via text and eliminated clumsiness or anticipation. When you send a text or make a phone call later, it will be a lot more natural.

In some cases, men take a lady's phone number and act unpleasantly or never message or call at all. A woman can become fearful with regards to whether you like her or intend to get in touch another time. If it appears you maybe like one of those Jekyll/Hide men who are cool in person yet scary over text, send her a good (short)statement with a lovely smiley, and you'll eventually set her mind at ease.

It gives her your name. If you've been at this for quite some time, you will develop an ability to remember everybody's name, since you get so used to meeting many new people that it simply becomes a normal part of you. Yet, most girls are not so skilled, and they may well forget your name no matter how much they like you or just how much you relate with them. This can downright embarrass a girl that a lot of times, she can not speak with you for the shame of it. Put your name at the end of that initial message, and you can get rid of the likelihood of her feeling stupid or ashamed.

To build the desired rapport, you may end off that first message, and not contact the woman at all the following day. You can later send a few rapport-building messages to make her comfortable talking with you.

Some basic tips on rapport-building texts include:

Be concise. Shorter messages get even more responses than long ones.

Remain Positive: Nobody cherishes a downer; bring considerable positive energy to your messages. Ladies must eagerly anticipate messages from you. Make them dread messages from the boring, life-sucking men ... while you illuminate their days.

Maintain it to a couple of messages. Unless you enter an incredible text conversation with a girl, you'll wish to keep it to about three to ten messages sent, generally.

It's alright to differ your response times, but do not reply a woman's texts too quickly than she responds to your own up until you make much progress, lest you risk looking like you're waiting by the phone for her reply with nothing better to do

How to Arrange a Meet Up with A Girl Through Texting

If you wish to build comfort and rapport with a woman, you can adopt a rough schedule like this: (a) preliminary message some hours after you first meet and collect her number; (b) rapport-building texts two days after the very first meet/number collection; (c) fix the date four to five days after the very first meet/number collection.

You do not need to speak to her for weeks before she's all set to meet you; you don't have to win her over. You just need to get her out.

There are three aspects to a meet-up message: (1) Be warm, (2) Ensure you offer value, and then (3) keep your eye on the ball. The ball being the eventual meet up..

The value you provide can be something loving or romantic with her, or it might be leading her to what she wants to do (which is to meet you). Don't get distracted.

Here's an example of what your conversation might look like as you forge ahead toward setting up a meet:

You: Jane, hi! Let's fix a time to grab a bite. Exactly how's this weekend looking like for you?

Her: Sure! This weekend is beautiful. How are you doing?

You: I'm good! Why don't we make it this Saturday at 2 pm. We can meet at Main St Avenue Exit 3 and go from there. Is that Cool?

Her: Okay!

You: Great. See you on Saturday!

That's all it takes. Keep in mind that when she asked how you were, you didn't give room for any distraction; you remained focus on the goal(the meet up). Remain focused and keep pressing for the meetup, smoothly, carefully, and smartly--. Plan a great date, and she's all yours.

The Three Common Texting Styles Used By Men

There are three forms of text messaging styles prevalent amongst men these days:

1. Clueless Boring Questions type of men

2. Endless Conversations type of men

3. Incredibly Witty and Interesting type of men

The above categories are listed in order of frequency, from the most to the very least experienced.

Despite being listed as the last, the Incredibly Witty and Interesting man is not all that uncommon.

Before we learn what to do to achieve good results with women out of texting, let's start with a consideration of what these three categories of men do, and why it does not work. Try not to be miffed if you know you're one of these individuals because if you are, you're precisely the target of this book.

Clueless Boring Questions type of men

To women, the most frustrating texter is the Clueless Boring Questions guy, hereafter abbreviated as CBQG. The CBQG has no clue on how to text women or what ladies would like to see in a text message. At no time has CBQG ever asked himself:

" If I was a girl, how would I reply to a message like this?".

He quickly assumes that all ladies are like him-- lonely and without many options. Thus, they must love to get messages from him, and they, therefore, ask clueless uninteresting questions like:

" What's up?" "How's it going?".

" How was your weekend break?" "What are you doing?".

" Do you have strategies?".

CBQG thinks that women enjoy getting texts like this from him. Besides, he 'd love getting texts like this from ladies. Of course, it must go both ways.

CBQG usually becomes distressed when ladies do not address his inquiries. He wonders why he does not get the desired rep.

He thinks ladies are difficult to understand and unnecessarily make things complicated.

He doesn't stop to understand she isn't there in person and doesn't have the same level of context and expressiveness from him as she would if he was there.

The CBQG doesn't also assume to himself that: "Lame people inundate most girls all day with lame requests. Most guys message, write, and say to girls the same ineffective things often.

This never happens to him, because CBQG recognizes himself so well that he knows that he's not ineffective. He assumes that everybody else needs to know this, as well ... even if he behaves the same way men, who are lame do.

" She'll know I'm not ineffective, also if I appear ineffective," CBQG thinks. "Otherwise, she's shallow and not worth my time!"

CBQG thinks that ladies must recognize his inner awesomeness. Women need to hammer out the lameness he shows outside to find his awesomeness inside.

CBQG spends several evenings alone, angry, and confused by how the world can be so cold and so confusing.

Endless Conversations Guy

Endless Conversations Guy, hereafter referred to as ECGis usually a CBQG that tidied up his act. Someday he considered his phone, which was devoid of replies to the messages he 'd sent, and says to himself:

" If I were a woman, how would I respond to a message similar to this?".... and in an unexpected insight, he recognized he had been doing it the wrong way. ECG is, you might, on a much more informed level than CBQG. He realized the need to involve a woman in dialogue. And also, he's recognized women don't desire to address stupid questions.

ECG still doesn't get much further beyond "engaging her in dialogue"-- and there he's usually stuck. ECG's conversations tend to look something similar to this:

ECG: Hey, Shirley, how did your weekend break go? I saw some close friends on Saturday, but yesterday was all just relaxing.

Girl: Hey, it was beautiful. My buddy from out of town came to visit, so we went to some restaurants and also saw some sights … that was all about it.

ECG: Cool, what sights did you see?

Woman: Oh, you know, he harbors, Sea World, just the usual things.

ECG: You know, I've been living right here for five years, and I've never seen Sea World. Everyone keeps telling me I ought to go.

Girl: I understand; I did not get to sight Sea World till I was 19, and also I grew up here. Isn't that ridiculous? But you should go, it's a lot of fun.

He doesn't know that the more time she spends with him in text chats and the less time she spends with him in person, the worse she feels about him, as researchers found studying young couples in 2014 (Luo, 2014). He doesn't realize most girls who engage in these with him are either (a) just doing it because they're also bored, or (b) just too nice not to send back a response. To him, it feels like he's unlocked the key to texting girls: just keep texting.

You can imagine how annoyed he becomes when a woman he's spent a lot of time within endless conversations always dodges his date demands-- and how perplexed he is to find, after weeks or months of discussions, that some other guy has eventually become her guy.

" How can this be?" ECG thinks, "I thought we had such special discussions!".He's bewildered ... it just does not make good sense. Why would she invest so much time talking with him and then decide to date somebody else?

The Really Interesting and Incredibly Witty Guy

Last but not least is the Interesting and Incredibly Witty Guy, henceforth referred to as RIWIG. Such a man is the next stage of evolution after ECG. He's a man who's discovered that endless conversations don't work. They can be tedious, kill his intrigue, and every man and his brother would engage in them fruitlessly.

RIWIG has a lot more experience with women than either CBQG or ECG. He does understand women react well to wit and choose interesting poor children to boring nice people.

" So," goes RIWIG's line of thinking, "what could be much better than being a poor boy via text?".

Most texting advice you'll see online or speak with close friends comes from RIWIGs. They've split the texting code, they'll tell you. They've identified just how to develop the feelings they desire in females ... wish, laughter, intrigue. Being really interesting and incredibly witty over text is the method of getting ladies drawn into you.

RIWIG leaves those guys in his dust. Just as CBQG can't hold a candle to ECG, ECG's odds to beat RIWIG in a text fight are about as good as a medieval pikeman's odds against a Navy SEAL with a minigun and a grenade launcher.

RIWIG's text conversations often tend to go something like this:

RIWIG: Oh, man, I just had excessive food. Never need to have eaten that last drumstick. Suggestions: gluttony doesn't merely make you fat; it's also quite uncomfortable.

Woman: lol ...where did you go, and why 'd you overeat?

RIWIG: Friend had a birthday party. There was far way too much to eat; I felt an ethical obligation to make sure there weren't unnecessary leftovers.

Woman: Did you save any for me?

RIWIG: Thought about it, but decided against it. You ought to be thankful I prevented you from withstanding a similar experience to mine.

Lady: But I want some too!

RIWIG: You know what, miss out on ... you are starting to get too hard now. The majority of ladies are a lot much more cautious when they claim things like that to me.

Lady: I'm talking about the food, duh!

RIWIG: That's what they always say ...

Girl: You are such a geek.

RIWIG: Hey, so [conversation continues]

This type of man is a big step up from ECG. But despite his extremely amusing and intriguing message text conversation, RIWIG is prone to some issues: (a) women will still frequently be dodgy about setting updates, and (b) when the dates are eventually fixed, the woman usually treats RIWIG as a prospect (i.e., she sets barriers to sex).

RIWIG thinks. "I was engaging, witty, sexy ... everything a woman looks for in a lover, not just a friend!

Being wittier and more enjoyable isn't the answer. The answer is something much simpler than CBQG, ECG, or RIWIG think it could ever be.

The Fourth Type of Texter

There's good news for the Clueless Boring Questions Guy, Endless Conversations Guy, and Really, Interesting and incredibly witty Guy. The good news relates to the fact that there's a fourth texter with a style they haven't tried out, thought up, or looked into yet.

And he doesn't need clueless boring questions. He doesn't require endless conversations. Heck, he doesn't even need to be all that interesting or witty. All you've got to do to use his style is be able to send simple text messages ... and tell the girl you want a date with her before you get her phone number.

If we had to give this kind of texter a name, I think it 'd be Just Get It Guy(JGIG). The style is more concerned about keeping things simple. The truth is, less "natural" media (like email and text messaging) are less meeting for people to deal with (Kock, 2004).

But a lot of guys still don't get it. They're still trying to mix in CBQG or ECG or RIWIG elements with this style of texting. Because those ingredients work great in other things you make, it's like taking a gourmet recipe and throwing in extra eggs and baking soda. The result is not something better. It's something worse.

CHAPTER TWO

Ground Rules for Texting

Text Messaging ABCs

The first step is to deprogram you from negative texting ways of thinkings, inadequate approaches, and misunderstandings.

These are things that make texting more challenging than it needs to be, causing men to send messages that simply don't work.

To do this, I'm going to give you the 8 "mental foundations" of texting you need to know. These foundations allow you to think about texting a woman in a reliable method that gets her ecstatic to see you and also all set to come out on a date with you.

#1: Faulty Models Are Your Responsibility to Fix, not women's.

You can choose to blame other individuals for your life, or you can head out and get what you desire. You definitely can't do both.

It'sblame and be miserable, or accept responsibility and go all out for what you desire.

As you go down the texting styles, you'll find out that the more advanced a guy's style is, the more he criticizes girls. The 'Clueless Boring Questions Guy' is the most awful. To him, nothing is his error.

The worse a man is with ladies, the more fault he sees in ladies. What's responsible for this phenomenon?

It's a symptom of defective psychological models.

Women give out phone numbers a lot. And they do not appreciate getting clueless monotonous questions from any person, even close good friends, family, lovers, guys, etc

So, simply imagine how a girl feels when she gets such questions like this from some person, she does not know all that well, or some guy she met in passing at the workplace or the bar or on the road or in class, even if he attracted her (in the beginning).

She would regard him as somebody who's a liability and not fun to have around. Her passion in him goes from whatever it was before the clueless monotonous inquiries began, right to absolutely no.

It's not ladies that are the problem. It's the texting style you have adopted.

If ladies don't think, act, or react the way you think they should, it does not in any way mean all the over 3.5 billion in the world need to change. What it implies is that your thinking pattern needs to change to suit the style women are.

This phase is about changing that version you've adopted.

2: Phone Numbers are Easy.

Inexperienced people view phone numbers as a big deal, which is one of the reasons they struggle so much with the concept of texting.

The problem is that, to girls, the phone numbers are not a big deal!

An inexperienced individual gets a girl's contact number, and it feels like an enormous success. Now he can relax. For all intents and objectives, he has found a sweetheart.

Except she does not see it in this way. For women, a telephone number is simply the START. And also, girls offer their names out regularly to individuals whom they never wind up talking with or seeing ever again.

You're not the only one asking her. Various other people ask her as well. And she says yes to several of them often.

Phone numbers mean nothing. They're nothing more than an opportunity. They are not a guarantee or an assurance of any kind.

If it assists, you can think about a phone number just as "Here's a way you can get me to meet you once more if you do a good work making me desire to.".

By doing this, when you start seeing numbers, you'll promptly start to understand why clueless uninteresting inquiries are a death penalty. That is, it's far much easier to say"No" to you over the phone than in the real world.

And if you're most likely to be boring and clueless on the phone, what's she supposed to do ... be delighted?

Giving out a phone number does not amount toa pledge; it's just a possibility.

3: Emotions Don't "Stick."

When you first exchange numbers with a girl, you could leave on cloud nine, dreaming about the fantastic future you'll have with her. Possibly you had an effective communication with her and genuinely connected with her on a quite deep level. Chances are, she's forgotten all about you.

Oh sure, she might still be considering you. You don't know that, and it's much better to think that she isn't. If she isn't, how then is she going to respond to your first text?

It's possible she's forgotten almost everything about you because it's more probable she's frustrated by other important issues in her life.

Is your message going to make her smile? Is it going to take a lot off her shoulders?

If I was truly angry and frustrated right now and I received this text arbitrarily from somebody I could barely remember, what would my reaction be? If the response is "a lot more upset and annoyed," you need to head back to the drawing board. Find something that much better stimulates the appropriate emotions.

Excellent-- that's a perk if she remembers you. You'll still send her a fantastic text, and she'll be even happier to hear from you. If she doesn't, if she's forgotten all about you and you eventually send her the right message, you still stand a good chance of taking her out on a date anyway.

4: People Want You to Help Reduce Their Cognitive Loads.

Envision you are anxious, you're worried like insane, running around trying to do a million things that you have pending. You wish to scream and punch the wall and pull your hair out just because you're so far behind on things. Then, you receive a random text message from some guy you met at a bar the other day who seemed like a nice person.

" What's up?" the text states

What's up??!! What, am I supposed to sit here and figure out what that means? Like, you simply desire to fire the crap, like I have time for that? Or, you want to ask me for some kind of favor, or want me to use something to you?

This happens to be the thought process of a very busy lady when she receives a text like that. It has been observed that ambiguous messages like "What's up?" are a few of the most mentally challenging messages of all. And that makes them amongst the least likely to get an expected response.

A lot of men want to get messages like this from women. Women do not appreciate receiving messages like this from men simply because such text messages raise mental loads.

The second a lady reviews a message like this; her mind puts whatever else on hold to ask itself: "Who is this? Is he going to ask me for something? Is he going to begin sending me lots of messages if I reply?

Much of the moment, her mind will just consider these and many other related questions and may just decide to put off her phone and never respond.

This is not because she's mean or cold or impolite or withdrawn or even indifferent; none of this is true. It's only because there is too much brainstorming to do, so she puts it off and then forgets about it. Or she remembers it once again later just to put it off once more.

Like it or otherwise, when it involves less-clear media like text messaging, the duty of making the sign of a text clear drops on the person sending out the message, not the one is getting it. It's on you to make it clear what you mean-- she isn't going to sit there and attempt to figure it out.

You should aim to be clear and make it very easy to respond to your messages. You must reduce mental loads as much as feasible.

Do not make her think. Do not make her wonder. Don't get her into giant open loopholes; she needs to invest substantial amounts of mental power on. That's an invite to overlook you, and you don't want her to see you as rude or socially stunted, either.

Smart individuals do not shift huge mental loads on other people using text. They make points easy. They take burdens off. You should, as well.

That implies, instead of "What's up?" you can say:

Hey Jane, I hope you had a great weekend. Mine was strong and restful, simply what I needed. When's okay for you to get hold of that sumptuous meal this week? Let me know when your schedule's clear, and let's fix it up.

No surprise what your motives are. No asking herself what you're after. No pondering on the best way to respond, and even if she needs to respond whatsoever. All she's required to do is tell you when her schedule is free or open.

It's very easy, and since it's very easy, you're most likely to get what you desire: a date!

5: You Must Not Take Your Eye Off the Ball

Think about it. How many of the terrific relationships in your life come from lengthy text message conversations? How many friendships? Sweethearts?

If you're like lots of people, the answer is this: 0.

That's because texting is an atrocious way to build purposeful relationships. This is not how to text ladies at all.

People still keep doing it. They do it in droves. And the reason for such is because their eyes are not on the ball.

If you've ever found yourself mired in lengthy text conversations, I bet you've never taken time to ask, "Where is this going?" And if you did, I'm sure your answer to that question would be "I have no idea!"

That is not the way to run a text conversation. It's not just how to run anything.

Imagine if a sailor takes out a ship into the deep blue sea with no clue as to where he was going. "I'm most likely to locate a gorgeous, unoccupied island available with a pirate's buried treasure, and I'm going to be rich!" he tells himself; "I just need to sail around sufficiently till I locate it!" After the triggers on his voyage, he might end up discovering an island in the vast sea with a few doubloons hidden in an upper body. It's much more likely he'll die at sea or return to port, bitter and more frustrated.

You practically always miss out on the mark when you shoot in the dark. With really couple of exceptions, texting is awful for building an emotional connection, getting involved in an actual discussion, changing a stranger right into a partner or fan, revealing your individuality and high qualities, or keeping or growing attraction.

You will certainly be missing the mark once more and once again if you use it for these things. You will not also get better at hitting the target in the dark. You'll simply throw away a lot of bullets, time, and patience.

No matter what happens, establishing a date should be the primary objective of your messages. Using it for anything else departs from your core goal and slashes the chances you'll ever make it to your aim of a phone call.

6: Girls Talk Because They Like to Talk

Unless you're exceptionally a talkative, I guess that you do not spend a good deal of time in long text talks with your male friends. Nor do you likely have these with a lady that's now your lover.

The majority of men just get into these long discussions with women they're pursuing. And such men assume that the girl understands what the bargain is. "So, once more, clearly she must know this, and also undoubtedly, her texting back to me is permission to continue with her!"

There're a whole lot of presumptions in there, and they're mostly inaccurate.

As socially sharp as many women are, they are incline visitors. They know you desire something when you message clueless dull inquiries or unlimited conversations or large quantities of really, intriguing, and extremely amusing stuff ... they simply will not understand what it is you desire.

Most ladies love talking! They will chat with you merely to chat. And they'll like it. Lots of girls will be delighted to message to and fro with you all day ... and not just you. They do it with their lovers. They do it with their friends. They do it with the other individuals that are chasing them and also texting them all day long.

You're there talking, thinking it's nearly in the bag, because she's so ready to chat with you. And she's there chatting with you, her friend, her lover, and other people.

This isn't the way to a lady's heart. It's merely a way to help her pass the day. You're losing if you invest time in long text discussions with women, and you will soon be much more useful as a texting friend than you are as a prospective lover.

CHAPTER THREE

Opening up the Hook

Now that you've got your structures established and you have learned the basics, you're all set to study the mechanics. These are the certain subtleties, the screws and nuts ... the core of how to text women and have it go the way you want it to, nearly consistently.

#1: Propose the Date Before You Ask for the Number!

It feels easier to ask for the number. If she says "no," all she's denying is giving you her phone number?

However, that's outrageous. If she refuses to give you her number, by extension, she refuses all future possibilities of you and her doing anything together, ever. That includes dating.

When you are trying to collect her phone number, you should request the date first! Not only does this make it much easier to get phone numbers from girls, it additionally makes things a lot easier when you identify how to correspond with her later.

Better still, it makes you look confident. If you had a chance to ask a girl out personally, then didn't, and waited to do it over message later, she may presume you lacked the guts to ask her personally and, therefore, not worth meeting again face to face.

If men began to ask women about dates before they asked for phone numbers, CBQGs, and ECGs would come to be extinct. And RIWIGs would end up being a threatened class.

All you need to do:

Her: [mid-conversation anywhere you meet] ... so after that, I entirely left there before things could get back at worse!

You: That's funny.

Her: I know. I thought I was going to pass away for a minute! That woman was insane!

You: Hey, I'm most likely to have to jet in a minute, but we ought to grab a drink or some food today or early next weekend. What's your routine like?

Her: Oh, I don't know, I'll have to have a look. I believe I'm free on Sunday.

You: Cool, I'll text you. What's your number?

Her: 619 …

Isn't doing this much easier than the big issues most guys make from trying to get phone numbers?

Moreover, doesn't that make it way more straightforward when you wish to text her later? I believe you understand specifically what you need to do now.

As a suggestion, you may open your phone right now and erase every number you took from ladies you didn't ask out in advance. Or, if you'd instead try out something before you remove those numbers, text every one of them now with something like:

Hey [name], I just stumbled across this trendy little coffee shop in [area] with the most impressive warm chocolates. I intend to take you there - want to get hold of a chocolate and a snack with me sometime this week/ next week?

Any of the ladies you get "yeah, sure" or a " how about we do XYZ rather" from, hang onto; you can surely work with that. Anyone, you get a "no, I really can't" or a "sorry, I'm busy" from, simply delete.

Now you're starting fresh and every number you collect from now on, before you collect it, ensure you've collected it in the context of doing so in order to set up and plan for a date.

Say goodbye to figuring out what to message her—no more pacing back and forth in your room just to decide what you should send us a text.

Now, you surely know what to say: you're going to message her to figure out when she intends to meet you.

2: Use an Icebreaker Text.

The longer you wait after getting a girl's number to text her, the weirder it begins to feel. There are a variety of "weirdness" elements that enter into play: she questions when you're most likely to text her, or she forgets about you completely; plus you build things up in your head and get uncomfortable, or you push things off so long that she wonders why you're texting a week later.

Solution? You just need to break the ice.

Starting a conversation provides you the liberty to be more natural later. The awkwardness of wondering whether the discussion will certainly be comfortable and also typical over text is gone.

Starting a conversation sets the tone for you to message women later on without needing to introduce yourself or remind her of when she met you. That's because you built those initial feelings while they're still fresh in her mind.

A simple icebreaker text resembles this:

You: Nice to meet you, new friend: --- Frank.

or

You: Glad to have met you: --- Frank.

You do not tell her you "like" her, qualify her (as in "You're a cool/amazing/neat lady!"), ask her any question, or suggest a date.

You do keep it short, use the word "good friend," if possible, sign your name.

Since this is just to break the ice and comfort her, you aren't one of these people that's in love and creating her novels now; it's brief. You relate from the beginning that you follow the Law of Least Effort, and you show her that meeting a new woman isn't a big deal to you ... like it is for many men out there that are quick to deluge women with lots of messages following the meeting.

Since you wish to confuse and captivate her a little bit, you make use of friends where feasible. Do you like her or not? She assumes you do ... and now you're using this ambiguous term. Ambiguity is among the properties of text, and it's one you can resort to your advantage. You use this, and she's assuming ... she's intrigued. The majority of guys specify spoken passion right away and also kill the excitement, enigma, and intrigue. Women don't want men like that ... they want men that'll keep them presuming and that will not let them know how the story ends-- keep up till it does.

If a lady appears very into you and appears to see you as far more exceptional standing than herself, you might choose to drop "friend" ... so as not to send her right into denial, assuming she can't get you.

If you do not include your name, and she forgets it, she's either going to feel uncomfortable that she's forgotten, and not react, or feel embarrassed that she's forgotten, and have to ask you. This is an all-too-common reason women use to comb guys off if they're on the fence.

Occasionally, you will get a girl writing "Who?" back after your initial message, and if it's just a few hours later, and if you've authorized your name. This is generally a brush-off attempt; do not react back by telling her who it is.

When should you send out an icebreaker text? About 1 to 4 hrs after meeting her.

You can sometimes go sooner, although 30 minutes is about the soonest you wish to do this. You're getting right into the awkward region ... so break the ice before, then if you wait a lot longer than 3 or 4 hours and do not worry about getting a response; you're texting to start a conversation, not open a discussion. You'll still get dates and enthusiasts from ladies who do not respond to your icebreaker texts. It's merely crowning achievement if they do respond.

3: Don't Wait Too Long.

You know those old dating guides that tell you to wait for about three days or a week before calling a lady? Throw those manuals in the garbage bin; they'll do you no good.

When you meet her, run things based on exactly how your interaction went. Use these plans if she was excited about you when you met her, send her a text to set up the date the following day, or perhaps that day if you met her in the afternoon or morning. You'll discover you can fix dates for the list below or the same day with women that were delighted to meet you. These are always your best bet... the emotions are fresh, the desire is warm, and you produce that speedy love that most girls dream of experiencing all their lives.

If she was beautiful towards you when you met her, text her 1 or 2 days later. Indeed, 1 or 2 days should be enough time for her to "make up her mind," whether she intends to see you again ... however, not all the time, she'll have shed rate of interest altogether. If you wait.

Remember the maxim on here: move faster. If you wait too long, some guy that knows this rule far better than you will beat you to the game. Or life may intervene with any number of other unexpected barriers.

Strike while the iron is hot, the orb on your own with an uneven blade (i.e., not such high chances to land her).

4: Don't Beat Around the Bush

If you lurk about and try to deceive girls into liking you and dating you, girls will respond subsequently and also slip around to try to trick you right into being platonic friends with them.

That's why all the "text her until she's ready for a date" techniques don't work that well. You cannot test your way into someone's heart.

You've to do that personally. If you're sending messages that do n't suggest a meet-up in the original text (in addition to an icebreaker text), you are eluding. Why? Because she knows you want something, but you aren't saying what it is.

Nothing concealed. No beating around the bush. Just some light pleasantries, and then you define what you want clear as day.

It's brief and straight to the point-- and also does not make her wonder at all what you're after. Females react better and even much more consistently to this than any kind of another texting style you'll ever before use (" respond" here suggests establishing a date with you, instead of becoming part of an engaging but ultimate productive text banter/conversation, which appears to be most men's concept of a woman being "responsive").

5: Keep Texts Short

Your very first message to kick off a new discussion can be a little bit of an exemption to this ... so that you have enough space to fit the pleasantries in preparation for the ask. Aside from that, your texts ought to not be much longer than the last you got from her.

That means if she sends you a text as follows:

Her: Hey Fred, didn't speak with you recently: What's up?

Don't send her:

You: Hey Jane, sorry I didn't respond faster! I was, in fact, very busy recently taking a trip to meet some new customers. It's truly amazing stuff but a lot of work. When I was in Vegas, though ... Wait up until you hear that one. I got to see the Cirque du Soleil! Anyway, what've you been up to? I hope all's been well. We still on for lunch this Thursday?

That's alright, and it's great stuff, but it's way too much as a reply to a brief text. If you've been excellent with her, she'll simply view it as you being passionate regarding a remarkable week. She'll see it as you attempting to force a connection if you haven't.

Rather, send her this:

You: Sorry Jane, I relied on my eyeballs recently: Tell you about it when I see you. Still lunch on Thursday, yes?

On the other hand, if a woman sends you a wall surface of the message, don't send her "Cool" or "Let's do it" as feedback. She'll feel uncomfortable and as though you aren't as curious about her as she is in you.

You want her to feel your passion level very closely match hers. To do that, you'll want to keep your text brief-- and comparable in length.

6: Ask and Share Something Personal to Relate

Imagine last week you met someone at a networking conference. Merely a healthy individual.

Then imagine it's a couple of days later on, and you've mostly forgotten about this individual. Now, he sends you a text. Which of these three is the most likely to get a "yes" response out of you?

Text A:

Acquaintance: Tim, wish to order that beer we discussed tonight?

Text B:

Acquaintance: Hey, Tim, how would that outing go? Intend to grab that beer we talked about tonight?

Text C:

Acquaintance: Hey, Tim, just how would that outing go? I've got one of those myself showing up ... what a discomfort. Intend to order that beer we discussed tonight?

If you're like the majority of people, and your time is spiritual (if your time is more of a free-for-all, have a look at the 1922 article: "Why I Quit Being So Accommodating"), your reactions will be something like a lady's response to the same texts if they originated from a man she met a couple of days informally back. So now let's use your answers to the above messages and also leap into the mind of a woman and also see if you can now know with her:

Her response to Message A:

" Wait, who is this guy? Do I want to give him my evening?"

Certainly not a reaction you desire. Her response to Message B:

" Is this man attempting to butter me up since he desires something?"

Also, not a response you want. Her response to Message C:

" This person feels like not a bad guy. I can manage a fast drink."

Now you're on the best track. What's the distinction? Text C is an individual and relates to you.

There's a unique formula here: (a) welcome her with her name (yes, this is crucial, informal texters); then (b) ask her how something in her life went; next off, (c) associate with that, and share something similar from your life; and lastly, (d) ask her to meet you, with a refined reminder that she agreed to.

The name is to reinforce in her mind that this is a personal message and not a mass text message.

Asking her about something private is to get her to begin relating.

Sharing your own experience in the same vessel as the inquiry is to end up connecting by showing her that the two of you are not so different.

Asking her to meet you is getting to the point, and also staying (in passing! Don't put it out directly, unless you wish to maintain that you do not believe she's most likely to say yes). That she's said "yes" makes her remember why she said "yes" and makes her a whole lot more likely to say it once more this time around. Keep it personal.

#7:Avoid Asking Too Many Questions/Irrelevant Questions

This's simple. Don't walk around asking ladies weird/irrelevant, or even whole lots of questions through message. A straightforward, how would your X go?" is a rule that makes things much more personal. A question like "Shall we grab that coffee we talked about today?" is necessary, so a woman doesn't feel like you're unilaterally trying to decide for her. "Let's order that coffee we discussed today" is too enforcing and is likely to lead to resistance.

Both of these inquiries are great.

They're just two concerns: (1) an individual "procedure" type inquiry, and(2) a "get in" kind query regarding the day.

Aside from those 2, that's it. No other questions-- everything else is unimportant.

You'll talk with her, even more, when you see her face to face. No deep diving using text, my good friend; much of its effect is lost without the body language and nonverbal communication.

8: Ignore Unhelpful Questions and Topics

Often a girl may be on the fence about whether she wants you as a friend or a day. When this is the situation, she'll commonly attempt to wedge distracting or purposeless questions or topics into a text conversation. She does this to slow points down or steer you away from "date-like" tasks and towards "friend-like" ones.

That resembles this:

You: Haley, how was your weekend break? I hope you had a lot of rest. I was very careless all weekend break, but often you need weekend breaks like that. Hey, so how about we get hold of that bite we talked on today? Allow me to understand what your routine's appearing like, and let's get the gears working.

Her: Hey, Will ... omg, my weekend was crazy. Way too much alcohol consumption Saturday night, never doing that once again, lol! Lunch? Allow me to inspect what I have going on this week. Oh, btw, did you read about the new club they're opening up midtown next week? It's called "Motown." We should be most likely to that! I have a buddy that says he can get tickets.

They feel like something's incorrect right here ... this woman seems to be calling the shots. It doesn't feel entirely best saying, "Sure, let's go to that club opening ..." yet they do anyhow, because they do not think they have a choice.

They did not ignore purposeless things. They invited it to the front door and also left that door open for even more to maintain gathering instead.

Why's this negative? If it's not clear why letting women lead, most likely to have dates, and things of that nature are inferior for seduction,

Next, when you get hit with unhelpful and distracting subjects, simply duck and also weave:

You: Haley, how was your weekend break? I hope you got a great deal of rest. I was super lazy all through the weekend ... but occasionally you need weekend breaks like that. Hey, so how about we order that bite we discussed today? Let me know what your timetable's looking like and let's get moving.

Allow me to check what I have going on this week. Oh, by the way, did you hear about the new club they're opening up midtown following week? I have a buddy that says he can get tickets.

There is such a thing as too much clubbing, believe it or not ...

Well, check your schedule and let me know if the day's good for you on grabbing the bite. I've got Wednesday and Thursday free at lunchtime, and Saturday free right up till 8 o'clock - allow me to know if any would!

If the lady just wants you as a friend here, you'll receive an adverse feedback on the date. She'll be "busy" those times and also try to reschedule for a few other times. She does this to keep the advantage and stay in control-- which is what she requires to good friend-zone you.

However, if she's on the fence, she'll come back and eventually inform you one of those times is fine.

Be prepared to have to do a kick-ass works getting some sexual stress made up when you meet her. And have your sprezzatura at full blast. Have both of these in place, and also, you can run away that "feasible buddy" mantle she's curtained around your neck. Simply ensure you scoot!

9: Use Interesting Language

This set's more difficult to teach. It's just best if you're well-informed and have a little experience writing. If you can pick fascinating, vibrant language out, it assists make your messages extra captivating.

A few vivid phrases to help you began:

" Shall we" as opposed to "Would you like to" or "Do you wish to" "Scoop you" rather of "Pick you up" (in an automobile, for a date, and so on) "Grab [lunch, a drink, etc.] or" Snag "instead of' Get" or" Have." Making use of verbs rather than nouns (e.g., "I napped" as opposed to "I took a nap").

Using active voice (" I got this" as opposed to "They gave me this").

Colorful language is simply more eye-catching, and also makes you more attractive, as well.

10: Vary Your Response Frequency.

When you're genuinely ... when you're involved in a hundred things socially, this isn't a problem. Or you've got six different women you're seeing. Or you're running your very own organization. Or you've got a million tasks to handle for works. In these cases, your feedback time varies typically. It'll be lightning-quick often, and glacially slow others.

This is optimum. Women respond best to guys whose reaction time is unpredictable, yet within a specific range. Now, if you constantly take a day to react to her, or it occurs way too much, she'll likely auto-reject. Do not go crazy.

Permanently, don't also go extreme in either direction. If a lady regularly takes an hr to write you back, don't constantly write her back in 10 minutes. Instead, compose her again in 10 minutes one-time ... and 2 hours the following.

Action times will undoubtedly tend to vary usually for many active people. If you observe that a woman: (a) always texts you back after the very same quantity of time (e.g., 40 mins), or (b) always messages you again after the very same quantity of time that it took you to react to her last message, you know she's playing video games with you. Don't call her out on it, simply ... be conscious.

And play her game back much better than she recognizes exactly how-- vary your response times and don't be foreseeable.

You'll keep her guessing-- and fascinating.

11: Make Seeing You face to face the only Way to Talk with You

Like we said we read earlier in this book, women speak because they like to speak. And as you recall, we likewise discussed that ladies want men to "just be(platonic) friends" with.

How does that affect how you text ladies?

Simple: you do not offer them what they're searching for over text. A woman wants a texting buddy? Excellent!

That's not you.

A woman wants a person to go into an in-depth discussion with over SMS? Amazing!

It just isn't you.

She desires somebody to send her great deals of texts and also make her feel special? Impressive!

But she'll need to discover a person else for that.

The only point you utilize SMS message for is getting ladies out to meet you IN PERSON.

If she can get her fill of you using text, the probabilities of her coming out to meet you go down substantially reduced.

If she genuinely likes you ... and if she truly wants to speak with you ... and she can not get that from you via text message ... and you will not speak to her on the phone much, either ...

She WILL meet you.

And also, when both of you exist, in person and also in the flesh, you can work your magic.

12: Leave Something Small to Cover, and Send a Pre- Meeting Text

It's finest to leave some tiny information out that you can cover later when you set up the real logistics of a date. While this isn't entirely needed, it's handy for your pre-meeting text.

You almost always intend to use a pre-meeting text for two reasons. The first is you comfort your day that, of course, you remember the location and time, and you will certainly be there. This nixes any opportunity of her reneging of fear of you disappointing up. If she plans to flake, the second is that you provide her the opportunity to offer you a heads up. If she's going to be late or not make it at all, this makes certain you do not squander your time going someplace.

A pre-meeting text with a relevant detail you didn't discuss earlier will certainly appear like this:

You: Hey, Cassie! Heading out in 10 minutes; must be there right at 2 PM. I'll meet you at the subway terminal's South Exit.

A pre-meeting text if you do not have any particular relevant data to cover will appear like this:

You: Hey, Cassie! Heading out in 10 mins; ought to exist right at 2 PM. If I'm the first one there, I'll order a seat inside.

Either of these works simply fine and both comfort her you're going. Both also advise her to provide you a heads up if she isn't going, so you do not squander your time (and even get angry/annoyed).

Suppose she does flake; indeed, after that, stay tuned. We'll speak about merely what to do two phases from now.

Texting When It's Been a While

In some cases, you could have a situation where you shed touch with the woman for a while. Whether it's because it really did not go anywhere or you just failed to remember, you stopped texting her. And she stops texting you.

After that, one day, you come across her number once more or remember her, and you think, "Man, that girl was cute. I would certainly like to see her once again." However, it's been so long, and she's most likely gone on. How do you come back in touch?

The way you do this is with what I call the "check-in" message. It's a way to get with a girl you've lost touch with. And you do it in a nice, natural method.

The Standard Check-In Text

The conventional check-in text message consists of these five elements:

1. Welcoming and her name

2. Apologies for why you've been quiet

3. The explanation that you've been hectic

4. Ask her exactly how she is

5. Ask her out and request her schedule

The welcoming and name we've already covered in the chapter on just how to message a woman. So let's speak about the other 4.

The thing you "did wrong" makes you high status and also vital, yet her reduced status and unimportant. And now you desire to make it up to her. If you do, many of the women you message will certainly treat it like it is the situation.

You've been active: here, you just desire to claim you've been active. You can mention the "why" if you like, yet it isn't needed. You just intend to provide her an understandable reason for your absence. This makes your check-in text conforming ... you were active, and also now points have cleared (and also you have time for her). This is the "piece of new details" component of a brand-new text conversation.

Ask exactly how she is: as you recall, "consideration" is just one of 4 components to include in a new cold message. Here you ask exactly how she is to reveal consideration ... and likewise since it's just a regular point for people to do that have not talked in a while. In this manner, if she has anything essential she needs to upgrade you on, you've provided her a social home window to do so.

Ask her out and request her routine: and also last but not least, you wish to solve the reason: ask her for her timetable. In this manner, she doesn't have to question what the message has to do with it. She doesn't require to ask herself what you're after. It's right there in the message. "Oh, alright-- he intends to order beverages and also capture up."

Here's an instance of what these aspects appear like all placed with each other:

Hey Gina! Sorry I've been silent these past six weeks; I wasn't neglecting you, I simply got so pounded with my projects that whatever beyond works got pigeonholed up until life returned to peace of mind once again. Anyhow, things have cleared up a little bit. Exactly how you been? Allow me to understand your schedule over the following week or two, and also let's strategy to assemble and capture up on points.

Non-Standard Check-In Texts

The common check-in text will be your text reset support. It's what you'll use most of the moment, with many women. What do you do in more extreme scenarios? A participant of the Girls Chase online forums asks:

To steam it down to brass tacks, what's needed is a method to produce a rate of interest from a woman we have just me when, a year to 18 months ago, number close, great chemistry, however, no day or same evening lay. They could additionally still be simple & cost-free and also living close-by and would certainly benefit from costs time with us and our recently-realigned viewpoints on exactly how to offer her what she desires & needs through enjoyable & frolicsome experiences.

What do you do in these more severe scenarios ... where you barely know the lady, or it's been far also long considering that you talked to them? Well, you need something a bit more severe than the normal check-in text.

Choice # 1: Clearing Out My Phone

Your very first option is to go through your phone and also clear out old phone numbers that did not work out. As you erase old names, try to find women you 'd such as to take one more shot with. When you discover them, text them this:

I'm sorry I have not chatted with you in forever ... I just got caught up with things, and did not get in touch. Listen, I was going through erasing old numbers, and wanted to touch bases once more and also see what's up. Want to get a coffee at some point?

You'll get some amusing responses back to this. Some of these women will only very vaguely remember you (or they won't remember you at all) ... and they simply assume from the tone of the text that the two of you must have been close ... in some way.

They'll meet up with you, both unconvinced and intrigued, and also they'll wish to remember just how you satisfied. Typically you intend to be semi-vague below. Don't attempt to jog their memories entirely. The past isn't essential. Just treat them, like a good old friend, be sorry that you haven't complied with up, and get on with things.

You can get an incredible boost occasionally with these girls. They'll seem like because they've known you for so long, they do not have to be as on-guard with you as they are with most guys. And also you still get the benefit of getting on their romantic and also sex-related radar displays ... unlike the majority of the men, they've recognized a long period and have long because put right into the friend area.

You're the long-lost person they never got with, but that goes back into their lives. It's a beautiful place to be.

Choice # 2: Leaving Town

If you intend to leave the city (or country), you can select numbers out of your phone and text this:

I got caught up with some points before, and never finished up adhering to up with you way back when. I don't recognize what you're doing, however, if you 'd such as to order a warm chocolate or an ice cream before I'm out of below, I would certainly love to see you one last time ... Shall we do that?

In my experience, this message gets you a higher reaction rate than Option # 1 ... that is, she's extra likely to react. The price she comes out on a date is lower than with the initial option.

If you've got 10 or 20 numbers that never went anywhere and you're on your way out, there's no reason not to use it. You might surprise yourself with what you get from it.

Aren't These Texts Too Long?

The Law of Least Effort simply says one of the most socially powerful guy is the one who gets the best results for the least amount of initiative. If you can send one text, and also perform in one text what it takes most guys several texts and also hours of texting and waiting to do, that's lower initiative.

And when it's been a while, you require a long message like this to get your message through. If you think you're going to message her, "Hey Gina, what's going on? She doesn't remember you, or you have not talked with her, so you're unnecessary.

→ "Oh, I see, he was active. → "Oh, he wants to meet up with me. Busy individual has time for me now, huh?"

You wish to roll from one of those feelings to the following before they have time to cement. You do not desire the message to end with her reasoning, "Who is this man?" since when your following message comes, you're now an enigma. You don't want it to be upright, "Why is he texting me?" because now you need to combat her suspicion.

The long text with every little thing in it breaks social convention somewhat. Yet it's so exuberant therefore sincere that no matter.

Ever get a thrilled, satisfied, yet likewise regretful long message from a girl? I have, lots of times, and you never care that it's long. You just catch the feelings she's sending over-- and those emotions feel excellent.

Example Text Conversation

While all this may seem made complex in the beginning glance, the tough work's all at the start. What excellent texting results in is vastly simpler message talks that line up days like dominos. All said and done, right here's an instant message conversation, start to end up, to provide you a feeling for what this appears like:

[an hour after meeting a new lady]

You: Happy to have made your acquaintance, buddy;-RRB- -[your name]

[two hours later on]

Her: Great to meet you as well!:-

[36 hours later on] You: Hey Sandy, how would the weekend break end up? I hope the rest of it was as remarkable as the starts were:-RRB- I wound up going to a pizza event with a number of people Sunday evening ... I haven't been to one of those given that I was 12. It was fun. And some wonderful pizza. On our bite today - when's helpful for you? My routine's rather open except Tuesday and Wednesday nights. Allow me to know what day's ideal, and we'll schedule it up.

[40 minutes later on]

Her: Hey! The pizza party appears fantastic! My weekend break was pretty cool ... Mostly simply recovering from Friday, lol. Just how's Thursday for meeting up? I'm complimentary most of the day.

[25 mins later]

Claim 1 o'clock in the afternoon? There's this impressive little café no one understands around on Green Avenue we can inspect out ... They have the most astonishing crepes around the globe.

[1 hour later on]

Her: That seems fantastic, let's do it! See you on Thursday!

[2 hours later]

You: Awesome - see you after that, Sandy!

[5 minutes later on]

Her: Hey, I'm running about 10 minutes behind. Sorry ...! I'm coming!

[3 minutes later on]

You: No, biggie. See you when you get right here!

Now compare that to the last ten texting conversations you had with females ... which are more challenging, and which are much less? The only challenging part here is in discovering the process. As soon as you've got it down, you can perform it flawlessly, successfully, and also continually ... and it's a point of pure elegance.

And also you'll rest there and take a look at the mobile phone of those poor ladies you're sleeping with or dating ... and you'll see the volumes and quantities of unaware dull concerns they get ... endless discussions they're mired in ... and really, incredibly witty and interesting messages they're inundated with ... and you'll drink your head at the individuals sending them.

" I used to be one of those people," you'll say to yourself. "But that ... was one more life.".

And after that thought will undoubtedly pass, and also you'll possibly never invest a 2nd idea on texting once more.

Most Significant Growth Areas for every Level.

Here are the most significant growth areas you can expect, depending upon where you're at with texting.

Development Areas for Beginner Texters.

As a novice, you'll wish to focus much of your interest in complying with locations:

Getting down timing. How quick or exactly how sluggish should you react? What days and at what times of day should you message? What type of message do you send out, and when?

Getting down structure. Your obstacle will certainly not merely be to get used to using the proper text structure, but to stick to it.

Anxiety overshooting. Eventually, you need to ask her out. Much better to find out to do it earlier

Development Areas for Intermediate Texters.

One of the most critical locations to concentrate on as an intermediate texter is:.

Getting down concision. The more concise you can make your texts (while still packing in whatever you must pack in), the much better.

Fascinating without being the fool. You wish to consist of fun, humor, and interesting little bits in your texts. Nevertheless, you do not intend to be the clownish entertainer. Just how you strike the best balance-- where you aren't dull, however also not over the top-- is just one of your essential difficulties at this stage.

Involving ladies properly. How do you get girls to, in fact, engage with you over text? Just how do you get them to take component? This is among your most prominent foci at this phase. As she takes part more, she does even more of the work to establish points up, and makes the courtship a lot more enjoyable for you.

Setting updates a lot more smoothly. Right here, you'll target elements like when and exactly how you schedule days, where you take women on dates, and just how you handle the ease of days. The far better you access this, the even more yeses you'll get, and also the fewer flakes you'll see.

Growth Areas for Advanced Texters.

The primary targets for the sophisticated texter to boost upon are:.

Reducing texting a lot more. What's the bare minimum of messages you need to send before you can get a lady on a date? The closer to this you get, the much less possibility you offer yourself to mess things up, and also the earlier you'll get her out.

Getting women to chase you and also seek you. Wouldn't it be wonderful if women worked to establish dates themselves? This is something you'll find yourself having fun with more at this phase (and starting to be successful at).

Getting very dominant and straight, both in exactly how you established your dates, and in how you deal with the more exceptional reasons of language framework in texts. The objective is to be powerfully dominant without being imperious. Attractive, instead than undesirable.

CHAPTER FOUR

What to do When She doesn't Text Back

Things That Lead to Unreturned Texts and also Calls

Think of a woman you that you such as, who you invested maybe 30 or 40 minutes talking to in your initial experience. She was captivating, attractive, precisely your kind.

Got her in your head?

Now, if you can, remember how you felt the initial time you called her or texted her. I nearly didn't call a girl who was to become my sweetheart for two years. It was just as well frightening to dial her number on the phone.

Guess what? Yep: that occurs to girls, also.

Now, it isn't always the reason. In reality, it's just one of four primary reasons we'll talk about that may trigger her to not respond to you. Yet nervousness and also pressure is one of the Big 4 Reasons why ladies may not meet.

This set's most likely the most unusual reason for a great deal of men, to make sure that's why I chose to lead with it. But there are three various other reasons, as well. The four reasons ladies may not respond to you are:

Also much anticipation/nervousness: if a girl likes you a whole lot, she can be "too reluctant to reply." She can place a lot of pressure on herself to do well with you ... or be too anxious to type out a reply or address your telephone call. She may want to speak with you, yet never finish up doing so.

Too much of a state-shift: this one's a little harder to get your mind around at first, so I'll utilize an instance. Claim you met an excited girl at an event, hit it off, and took her phone number. She will look at your message and think to herself, "I cannot talk to him right now; it's too many words ..." and after that just never get back to you.

She wasn't all that interested: this sometimes occurs to every person. Stand up to the lure to connect every no-response to disinterest. This is what many people do (" I guess she didn't like me besides"). It's quite often one of the various other three reasons that's to criticize. Occasionally it is just that she had not been as interested as she appeared. It takes place.

Of these four reasons, # 3 and # 4 are the most convenient to fix.

Number 3 (poor closings) you repair when you get your closing structured. Make use of these suggestions and get even more technique choosing closes, and you'll begin to self-correct and get smoother and even more natural with time.

Number 4 (she simply isn't interested) you repair as you come to be more in harmony with

the signals females are providing you You expend more familiar with just how to inform a woman wants you. Then, you plain and straightforward don't take call details from girls you know aren't that interested.

Because they like you,) is harder to correct, number 1 (women who're as well nervous to react. You need to minimize uneasiness and make the most of comfort while you're there in person with her ... plus, you've got to make sure that the call you have with her later is hot and friendly. She has to feel comfortable reacting to you, above all.

Number 2 (ladies that have a large mood shift in between the time you meet and the time you message) is the hardest to deal with. The objective is that when such a lady gets your text or phone call later, when they're in a much less spicy mood, it won't also feel tough for her to respond.

These four adjustments might need you to upgrade you entirely.

Communications with girls … specifically, if you're an energetic, high-energy individual.

Fortunately, however, exists's a faster way around all these discovering contours. That shortcut is …

Spend Less Time with Girls and Get Them RespondingMore

Less time invested with a girl before you go for her call details does something unique for you. First, it allows you to evaluate out girls that aren't a lot right into you. It additionally lets you cut out the negative stuff: women that get so into you they're too terrified to speak to you later on; girls who get used to talking to you in a too- various power degree from their current power level; and bad closings to your communications with women.

Said another method, less time upfront has to do with as close to a magic bullet for the"women not texting back" trouble as you can get.

The ladies that are right into you right off the bat aren't time wasters. They may well take pleasure in the long conversation they have with you ... or perhaps they're simply attempting to be polite with someone that took the time to method and talk to them.

A woman's smiles, giggles, and talks with you are reactions. Her relocating someplace with you, or providing you her number when you ask for it quick ... those are a couple of examples of results. Outcomes are what you need, no matter how promising (or otherwise) your reactions might be.

You get an actual result when you ask for the number quickly. The ladies that like you will gladly give their own. The ones who aren't so inclined will wait, or refuse outright.

Expeditious means to sift the wheat from the chaff.

When a Girl Doesn't Text Back

You met a woman, ended up with her number, today you've called or texted her and she hasn't responded. What to do?

When a girl doesn't message back, or when a woman does not call back ... first, do not panic. It's not the end of the world. It doesn't imply you've lost her completely.

It just implies she hasn't returned to you yet.

Determination. It's the difference between the guys that want it and get it, and

the guys who do not. There were people I mentored who would have women disappear and act indifferent, but they would certainly just continue. Eventually, the ladies would certainly re-emerge, agree to meet, and also ultimately wind up in bed.

Persistence via text or phone can work wonders ... But it's essential to linger in a cool, laid back, socially savvy way. Do not get mad at ladies for not responding.

Instead, here are some things to bear in mind ... so you continue in the type of intelligent, appealing means probably to make a lady wish to chat to you once again:

Don't get accusatory or mad. Yes, it may appear impolite that she hasn't responded yet ... you're an unfamiliar person! She does not understand you from Jack again, and also doesn't understand what a remarkable guy you are. Angering is 100% guaranteed to scare her off. Abstain from anything like, "I don't understand why you're so aloof."

Do not get whiny. Simply as poor as mad is sad: whiny, complain-y males are a.

Huge turnoff to every girl out there. You would not care to get something like that from a woman ... and also a girl will care even much less to get something like that from a man.

Do be nonchalant. "Hey Karen, figured I 'd drop you a line since we have not attached in a couple of weeks. I just returned from the East Coast and the beginning.

- Chase" Treat the circumstance as if no one is to blame, and also the 2 of you are just reconnecting after a little time off, merely busy with your points. Calls and texts are not the area to air grievances or bandy about poor emotions. That's the kind of point that makes a lady desire to select up the phone and talk to you ... because she likely does not get it anywhere else in her life.

DO refrain from being also entertaining. "Just saw the most impressive motion picture today!" "OMG, assume my head is going to take off, you'll never think what just took place to me ...!!!" Anything like that is no good. That sort of stuff is perhaps alright three or four messages right into a conversation with a lady. To send that as a cold message, as your text opener, drips of try-hard reaction-seeking. Worse, in my experience, it rarely works. And also, when it does work, it gets you to focus from curious girls, not interested ladies. Stick to regular stuff, and you'll do great.

Don't be worried about providing a girl a little time off if she doesn't respond for a while. My regulation of thumb is something like this: she doesn't reply when: provide her a day of radio silence. She doesn't respond twice in a row: provide her 2 - 3 days of radio silence. She doesn't respond three times in a row: offer her a week of radio silence.

If she's still silent, you might try something bolder, depending on the scenario. There's no unique, proven method to reengage a girl who isn't reacting. It's most likely to vary by the reason that she does not respond, to begin with.

If she's as well timid, a beautiful, cozy voicemail could work ... or reduce.

Your messages if you've come across regarding entertaining, gamey, or insincere.

On the other hand, if it seems like excessive of a state-shift for her, share some more normal information of your life and inquire about hers. Often that's all it requires to assist her in seeing you as more "human" ... and also get her to respond.

When Texts Don't Work, Use Phone Calls

In some cases, You've Got to Change the Medium.

I wish to discuss a fun little method. This tech helps you get in touch with a way to get somewhere with women that don't react well.

This method is, simply, changing backward and forward in between texting and also calling.

Now, if you've done things right from the beginning with a lady, you won't usually require to utilize this. A great impression, mounting for the day before you get the number, after that strong message video game to establish points up ... that's generally most likely to do whatever you require it to do.

Generally, if you need this method, it's since you've done glitch: you made a weak very first perception, you didn't make it clear you desired a date with her, or it can be your texting was weak.

She has just established a bad criterion and secured negative feelings to messages from you. Sometimes a girl might get it in her head that "XYZ point is difficult" (like when you fit on her routine) for reasons she isn't aware of (anchoring).

For any type of such a scenario, you have one neat device in your toolbox: just vary the means of correspondence. In this phase, I'll show you how to do that by switching between texts and also phone telephone calls.

Objections to Text/Call Splitting.

There are three main arguments to text/call splitting, so let's address those.

1. If she does not react to my messages, why trouble?

2. Isn't making a call intrusive?

3. Isn't using telephone call dated/outmoded in today's day and age?

1: Why Bother?

This objection is no different from anything else with conference ladies: "Cold approach is hard. Why bother?" "Men need to lead. Why can't I await ladies to lead?" "All this 'find out game' stuff is a great deal of work. Why not just be myself instead?" The solution here is the same: because it works.

Not everyone intends to do every little thing, which I comprehend. Yet if you're an individual who won't use text/call split because he does not wish to, after that whines that females do not text him back ... well, that's simply foolish.

Some individuals view such strategies (where you remain to comply with up with a lady that isn't bursting at the joints for you) as the chase. Sure, they are … if you're doing them incorrectly; however, you can say that of anything.

Picture this: an active, important male satisfies a gorgeous woman. He messages her to meet up several times, yet it does not turn out. Meanwhile, he's taking place dates with various other girls, also.

One day on his way to the gym, he gets his phone and calls this woman. She answers, they chat, he establishes a day with her before the telephone call ends, and also after that, he hangs up and goes on about his day.

Chasing? No.

This is how you'll be using this strategy.

2: Isn't Making a Phone Call Intrusive?

Not as invasive as what you'll be doing to her in the bedroom.

To a certain level, you wish to be considerate of a girl's time and not place way too much stress on her beforehand (before you're fans). A minimum of this is precisely how you wish to kick points off. I'll inform you of a secret, though ... not all females are produced equal.

Some ladies desire a guy that'll leave a minimal footprint on their lives-- one that'll make things simple and low pressure for them, and take up little of their time. Other ladies desire a male who's most likely to impose himself on them in smart and eye-catching means. They prefer a man that will certainly require them to take note of him.

The wonderful feature of the text/call split technique is that it begins out: "I'll be awesome, and also we'll do this in an unimposing way." If she does not respond to that method, it switches over to: "Hey, I'm vital, so let's set this up.".

Dating itself is an invasive process. You intrude on her time, invade her thoughts and desires, and finally horn in her body. If you're (excessively-- a little is great) stressed regarding being "also intrusive" with a woman you intend to copulate with ... well, possibly it's time for a little asshole training.

Additionally, remember, some girls like telephone calls over message. By beginning with the message, then moving to the phone if it isn't working, you enable yourself to cover both groups.

3: Aren't Phone Calls So 20th Century?

There's additionally this objection that asks: "Who makes a phone call anymore?" The answer, of course, is "active individuals." Call just is just the most beautiful interaction medium for a particular sort of talk.

When you try to set something up over message, and it isn't working, the just.

Individuals that maintain texting are trainees with excessive time on their hands and other individuals that don't have a lot of things to do.

That does not indicate YOU have to just text ladies in university or ladies with also much time on their hands. They recognize and appreciate an excellent phone telephone call from a hectic male as a lot as anyone else.

The hectic person simply calls. As opposed to 100 text and half a day of inputting and also waiting, he can complete everything with a 2-minute phone telephone call.

You will be active if you are successful with females. And the type of male women find appealing are those who are busy. Among things you'll discover is that the busier you get, the much easier dating gets, and it's not a coincidence. Busyness works as a sort of implicit preselection. If it's evident, you do not have a big amount of time for her (without you being "fake hectic"), that states advantages regarding you. It states you reside in abundance and have points that are very important to you in your life.

Another option to the text/call split is the "round in your court" message (we'll speak about it in two phases). You can utilize one of these methods, or both of them. If you've now done a few phone telephone calls, and she still will not come out, you will want to do a "ball in your court phone call" call rather than text ... yet we'll chat regarding that later on.

Another group of individuals that choose calls to messages are lonely individuals. You'll locate some girls might be slow to respond or non- receptive over text, however really receptive over the phone-- particularly if they are sad, lonely, or depressed. Phone is simply an extra individual tool, and one that's much better for individuals who prefer a more personal touch.

Phone calls are as great now as they always have been IF your phone video game is good (same IF as it's constantly been). Like anything, this is a skill you have to educate, and it takes a little time. If you aren't used to chatting on the phone, it can feel like phone calls aren't working that fantastic for you, because they aren't yet.

Ways to Call/Text Split.

These days, I suggest you typically start with texts. But not constantly. We'll cover scenarios where you desire to lead with a telephone call a little later in this phase. Normally, you will lead with texting. That's because it's simple, low stress, and the learning curve's much shorter than call.

You only require to be great at standard logistics-handling messages to get dates with a text video game, supplied naturally; you're doing whatever else right before you get the contact number. So it minimizes the level of skill you require to get dates, which is what long-distance document is everything about: get her out in individual with you.

You need to type only utilize telephone call nowadays when one or even more of the following holds: (a) you sent her icebreaker and follow-up texts, and she did not respond; (b) you tried to establish a day(s) through message, and she flaked or didn't meet; (c) she has continuously dodged day demands or is challenging to select.

In each of these cases, the phone telephone call ups the ante. Continuing to text when she's incredibly elusive placements you as the chaser. She may call back; she may not.

My general referral on when to use text/call splits vs. the ball-in-your-court message is: if you're "meh" regarding the woman, toss the sphere in her court; if you 'd like to see the girl, text/call split. You'll often tend to discover phone calls have a far better percent than ball-in-her-court texts if you're excellent at phone video games. Phone calls are additionally a heck of a whole lot more time effective.

That indicates, if you don't have a great deal of time (say, you'll leave community soon), OR you simply wish to get this girl ASAP (if she'll be off the market soon ... or if you just really like her), there's no point claiming you do not care-- and jumping her the "it's in your court" text-- when you do care. You also do not need to wait two weeks for her to decide she desires to date you, either.

If you want her-- and texts aren't working-- after that call her. Right here's how you do that in 4 steps.

Action # 1: Good Text/Impression Game.

How likely she is to answer your phone call is straight tied to exactly how reliable your text message game is, and just how excellent a very first impression you made. If your text video game was unique and also your first impression was good, she's going to tend to desire to answer your telephone call.

Women are regularly looking for good emotions. They will invite you into their lives if they watch you as somebody who can provide these. That means: do not simply slouch with your messages and think you'll call her if it does not exercise. You still require a good message game. Without that, she's less most likely to answer your call.

Action # 2: Time It Properly

Particularly if you're new, it's essential to provide her enough time to react to messages.

Some ladies take hours to get back to you; some can take a day. This does not always suggest they aren't interested; although, if she does not respond in 3 or 4 hours, you possibly have work to do as soon as she's on the date. It can merely suggest a girl's busy, or keeps her phone on silent, or doesn't check messages a lot. Believe it or not, there are ladies around that don't check their messages often ... mainly professional ladies or others with a lot going on.

So do not fall into the catch where you text a woman, she doesn't respond right

away, and afterward, 90 minutes later, you're calling her. It looks clingy and also frightened, as you rested around looking at your phone, and even called when you did not listen to back.

Instead, a joint development could look something like this:

1. Meet the lady

2. [3 hrs later] Ice-breaker message

3. Follow-up plus date-ask

4. Phone call with date-ask

5. [IF no date/ evades-- 3 days later on] Text invite to something different

6. [, if no date/ evades-- 2 days later] Bonding call without any date-ask

7. [3 days later] Phone call with date-ask

8. [IF says no/ evades-- 3 days later on] Text welcome to something various

9. [IF states no/ dodges-- that evening] Ball-in-your-court phone call

That's five days invite in two weeks without feeling rushed, packed- in, or try-hard. That's respectable. It's great because it filters for as lots of variables as feasible: perhaps she doesn't desire a day eventually you ask; however she does on an additional; possibly she does not like among your date suggestions, so you cycle via others; maybe she does not like one medium (messages), yet enjoys to get a call.

You provide in your room to find an angle that works for a lady where previous perspectives did not make when you switch over tactics up.

Action # 3: Keep It Fresh

You want to talk about some topics you've previously covered ... while at the same time presenting new details, ideas, and stimulations. Do not be the man who invites her to coffee on Monday, gets a "Not right now, thanks," after that messages her again welcoming her to coffee on Thursday ... after that messages her once again on Sunday to welcome her to coffee once again.

Rather, be the individual who welcomes her to coffee on Monday, then welcomes her to an art gallery opening on Thursday. That's for two reasons: it provides you the opportunity to strike on something she'll claim "yes" to, and it makes you much more fascinating: "What's Scott going to recommend this time?"

For the call, comply with the call overview and also make certain you have a.

The current narrative prepped to go. You will not always need it, yet it's convenient to have resting there at-the-ready. You can introduce right into your tale to warm up the discussion up if she does not delve into the conversation right away.

Action # 4: Texts for Logistics, Phone Calls for Bonding.

Maintain this regulation in mind: the text is for logistics, phone telephone calls are for bonding.

If you had a fast communication when you initially met her (e.g., a 2-minute number close) ... or you didn't have the best communication. After that kind of stumbled the follow-up over text ... you might require to do a little bonding before she feels comfortable enough to meet you. That's where the call can be found in.

Don't use texts to attempt to build connections, as a result of the lack of context. You can joke about messages, and you can set up logistics, but they aren't excellent for much else. Your sexy bedroom voice plus 10 mins speaking to her on the phone can be enough to swing a great deal of ladies from "on the fencing about you" to "completely on board.".

The greater context of call likewise makes them extra immune to negative anchoring. If she begins connecting negative emotions with your texts (" He's too aggressive" or "His texts are boring" or "He always messages me at bothersome times"), it's easy for her to secure these emotions to you and not desire to respond to. However, with a telephone call, specifically, if you're proficient at phone video games, it's straightforward to infuse interest, selection, and power. These make it simpler for you to anchor stable positive emotions ... insomuch that even if she declines a few days, or if you don't always call at convenient times, you still provide energy that makes her intend to answer your call.

If she appears unclear regarding you over text, or she's dodgy, call her. It ups the stake (" Okay, let's get major about this") and reassures (and re-attracts) her in means texts can not.

Call/Text Splitting Caveats.

There are some caveats to what we've laid out in this short article, also. These are that you have to call FIRST if you're time-pressed or if she's clearly warm for you and that when you've introduced calling, any type of ball-in-your-court interaction has to more than a call, not text. Below's what these two caveats mean.

When to Call First.

The regular policy is: lead with texts, comply with (if needed) with a telephone call. Often you don't have time for texting and also waiting, waiting, and texting.

When you're simply around for a few days, for instance, texting can murder your odds to see a lady once again. Even if she intends to meet you, by the time you get it all arranged, you may already be on your train or trip out of there.

In this situation, also, if leading with a phone call possibly isn't the social standard in itself, still do it. If your phone game is good, it won't matter, because as soon as she's on the phone, she'll be enjoyed to talk with you again.

Also, in some cases, you meet a lady, and you can inform she's very thrilled to meet up with you once again. When this holds, it's commonly better to lead with telephone calls over texts.

Leading with calls brings her back to a more productive interaction channel, which is what she wants. Ideally, she intends to be with you, not be talking with you at a distance. Telephone calls are a lot closer to really being with you than messages are. You can call, advise her what she's so ecstatic regarding, and get her to meet up, with any luck pronto.

You might face the scenario where a lady is piping hot for you in-person, then you start to massage her, and she grows cool. And also after that you call her once again, and she's warm again. What's taking place below is the texting is a disappointment for her. She does not desire to connect with words on a screen that represents you. She wishes to connect with you. When you have ladies that like you, you might find you're much better off with phone calls instead of texts.

What happens if the initial telephone call doesn't get you a day? No worry; just usage.

Text/call splitting, and remain to switch it up.

What Medium to Use with Ball-in-Her-Court Messages.

Usually, the ball-in-her-court message is done using a message. Nonetheless, if you present a call, you need to do this via phone, not message. The reason why is because phone telephone calls are a more severe, a lot more "genuine" tool than text.

If you're now talking to her using telephone call and you provide her an incredibly "real" message like "When you've got time and intend to grab a beverage, drop me a line and let me understand" over text, it comes throughout as a little afraid. Oh, so he can speak with me over the phone about ABC and also DEF; however, he can't tell me I'm preventing him and ask me to allow him to know when I'm prepared over the phone? Scaredy feline!

Do not ask her out and additionally offer her a ball-in-her-court message in the very same phone call; it appears spiteful. Do not do this:

You: ... blah blah. Anyhow, we should order one of those mojitos you keep chatting about-- want to do that this week?

Her: You know, today's active for me. I do not assume I can.

You: Okay. Well, it appears like you're always pretty active lately. Inform you what; I'm not so efficient the entire chasing-you-around point, so why don't we leave it off for some time, and then when you've got a long time, you can drop me a line and let me know when you intend to assemble?

Feels like you're sort of whiney or bitter right here, does not it? That's since you're instantly complying with the rejection up with the ball-in-your-court message. This is various in text. Since a text message is much less individual, whatever feels much less severe. Her decreasing your day isn't that big of a deal, simply like you tossing the ball in her court isn't one either. So you can follow up a turned down day request with a ball-in-her-court message. It does not seem like you're stating this just because your feelings are harmed.

However, for the call ball-in-her-court, you require to make points differently. Rather, ask her out utilizing text, and if she dodges/rejects, call her that night and have a short (2 or 3 min) phone call ... then ball-in-her-court her.

That resembles this:.

[2 to 3 mins of tiny talk/chit-chat]

You: Yeah, so anyway, it looks like you're incredibly busy/tough to meet!

Her: Yeah, you know, I work lengthy hrs, and this work I'm on today is drawing up all my downtime.

You: I entirely understand. I had a project like that about four months ago. It was fun, yet my social life just vanished. Hey, so, I don't intend to keep calling you and texting you and distracting you when you're so active, and I'm also dreadful at the entire chasing thing, as you can most likely inform. [pause; allow her to laugh] So I'll quit bugging you for now; however, I 'd like to meet up with you at some time and stop being unfamiliar people over a phone line. Inform you what, when you get some spare time, fire me a message or give me a telephone call and let's assemble, that work?

Say your farewells and get off the phone.

Keep in mind the distinction in tone and also message structure from the ball-in-your- court text message. It's a lot more conversational here, and you put more time in to communicate, "I get where you're originating from, and I comprehend." That's since the phone is a richer tool, and also, you must make it clear you're not saying this because you're starting.

The reason you call her that night steams down to a fundamental property of operant conditioning. That is, favorable punishment (eliminating something she enjoys) works finest when it closely follows the negative behavior it penalizes.

In this case, her cleaning apart yet one more day request is the bad behavior. The decisive penalty is that now you're going to wait for her to call you. And also, you aren't going to call her and provide good feelings, happiness, and enjoyment any more.

If you do this 2 or 3 days after being rejected, or even the next day, the sensation has waned, and also, she won't link the penalty to the habits. That makes her less likely to assume "Oops-- I created this; I did glitch ... I would certainly better fix it if I desire the fellow feelings back." Rather, she's more most likely to believe, "Hmm, I presume he's simply offering up," or "Maybe he found somebody else; I need to carry on, as well possibly.".

If you need to use the ball-in-your-court telephone call, time is essential.

CHAPTER FIVE

Myths about Women

There is much disinformation in our society relating to dating. That's why it's essential to utilize your mind and to trust your intestine.

While the full description about various myths would undoubtedly be the subject of a whole different other books, I would certainly still such as to briefly clear up why the individuality qualities and activity reasons referenced over tend to lead to successful dating.

Females have standard needs-- simply like guys. Nonetheless, they are different from male needs. Culture also places a lot of limits and stress on ladies, and males need to recognize that.

Females are not seeking males that play games and are usually uninterested in playing games themselves, despite what prominent society would certainly have you believe.

As women and men, both advance, communication, and also partnerships will become increasingly more healthy and balanced and also meeting. That's why you might require to throw away several of the preconceived notions regarding ladies that you've been force-fed all your life by family, buddies, associates, or TV.

That's why it's so crucial for you to be helpful and charitable for your girl. It's a whole great deal more challenging for women than for men to advance financially. That claimed, it does not suggest that you require to end up being a doormat for a lady that does not care to do anything in her life.

Even successful women require a man! This indicates that you still need to embrace some of the traditional works while being open-minded and encouraging to the woman's life, her objectives, and her challenges. Yes, this implies a little bit more work, but it features better advantages.

While a few of your pals might claim that you need to concentrate on amount instead of quality, in the long-lasting, it's a losing recommendation. Why? Since while others develop and expand in partnerships, consequently brightening their skills for future encounters, you'll be left behind.

Experience and technique are vital. You need to see what helps you and what does not. This is what will make you a hero over time.

While being a gamer sounds attractive to numerous guys, usually, they recognize that there is no actual compound to it-- on their own or for the females. It's a lot easier to claim what your goals and objectives are in advance and also to have a true partnership. It will be a great deal for both.

The 5 Most Damaging Mistakes About Texting a Girl

Texting ahead of time

This looks like a no brainer, but it is a refined point. Discharging off a message right after meeting a person, typically is not a good concept. Also, if they are throughout you, you still show some restraint. Waiting a day or 2 to get in touch with for the very first time shows emotional maturation and power. Leaving the texting conversation initially or not texting as usual as she interacts that you remain in need. Something as simple as this often plants a seed of uncertainty, which will undoubtedly draw her as well you like iron to a magnet.

Being sexual

Texting too often, as well as quickly is the most typical texting mistake, yet being excessively sexual is the most damaging when texting ladies. What a lot of people do not get is that ladies have an integrated hereditary concern of guys that can be caused by a sneeze.

If you have not created sufficient convenience in the connection, sending out even the slightest sex-related message will trigger her "RUN AWAY!" impulse. She will undoubtedly perceive that the sexual is your only passion, and if you are creepy in the slightest, it's around.

To double up on this concern, no woman, also the most promiscuous lady (think me I have evaluated this), refuses to be regarded only for sex. It may be 100% real that she wishes to breach you to the same degree, yet you can not be the one open this door. When discovering exactly how to text a woman, make her feel secure first, and also, I assure you if there is attraction, sexual intimacy will adhere to.

Being overly aggressive/cocky

There is a big distinction between being cocky/funny and just being a jerk. He got on a high from his previous success, yet he took it too far with this lady.

The trouble is when you run into a lady who can't hang with this or just is unaware as to just how to react. If you are playing tennis with a 5-year-old, lob the damn round, do not send it flying at their face.

It is also lovely/boring.

I see this at all times when I show people exactly how to message girls. They do not recognize just how to message a girl in a means that produces stress, develops tourist attraction. Playing it risk-free is very easy; however, it gives the least return on your efforts. In various other words, if you gamble at nickel ports, you will never get the big payout.

Him: Hey, wow, it was wonderful to meet you last evening.

Her: Yeah, you appear lovely.

Him: I am, yet you are not just sweet, however, so cute!

Her: Wow, you are not so bad on your own (She is flattered, however gently repulsed).

Him: So cutie, what are you doing tomorrow, love to get you dinner.

Her: Thanks a lot but I need to ... (Laundry my hair, wax my base, etc.).

It isn't because ladies like jerks a lot more, yet it is because the shake develops stress and that stress is sexy. I know you have experienced the same point with that truly wonderful, actually charming lady you discarded. When texting ladies, you should push the limits, you must be fascinating, or you will certainly never be sufficient.

Connection warnings.

This is more of a girl point to draw, but I have gotten plenty of e-mails from men who have broken this. Here are instances of offensive partnership ultimatum messages:.

Hey, I genuinely like you, and I would love to understand where this is going?

If I text you, I would genuinely, such as a message back faster, seem like you do not care.

I feel like I am the just one working on this relationship.

I am not cool down with you having so many person pals.

I truly like you, and I don't want to play any kind of more games.

All of these texts are interacting, "I am weak, I require reassurance that you care, you have even more power than me, I am envious, and also I am imitating a woman." , if you write this kind of text, you require her right into an extra male duty. She will act appropriately and run away, just like you would. Allow her to relocate in the direction of you initially, then inform her you feel the same. Always keep the equilibrium when texting women, continually be the one in control of your emotions.

Also though many guys assume they understand just how to text women to build attraction and rate of interest, many of them regularly dedicate basic errors that finish up murdering any type of attracting the lady might have had.

The awful part is, these are easy errors that could easily be stayed clear of. There are three very typical yet extremely deadly blunders that people often make.

I'm most likely to inform you what they are and, likewise, just how to fix them. See if you are guilty of a few of these mistakes and make sure to do them once again exceedingly.

OK, below we go …

Harmful Text Game Error # 1: NOT Waiting Until You Get A Reply Before Sending Her Even More Messages.

You need to never send out a girl several text without her very first reply back to your original message. The only exemption is when your first message did not get provided, and also your phone offers you a mistake message.

Various other than that, you ought to always wait up until she reacts to your very first text before you pound her inbox with even more messages.

Why, you ask?

Because refraining from doing so only interact with her that you are hopeless and clingy. Similar to a lot of the lovable losers that she 'd engaged with in the past.

This is a substantial turn off for women!

It decreases your worth and gives her power over you. The more you maintain texting her without her replying, the much more it emerges that she is the prize, and you are merely asking to talk to her.

Just keep in mind, you merely me this woman. Don't offer her the impression that you are now selecting the wedding celebration dress.

Harmful Text Game Error # 2: Making Your First Text To Her Boring.

The very first text message to a woman you simply me is one of the most crucial texts you will certainly ever send her. This is the text that will mainly determine whether she react back to you, so don't make it uninteresting!

Most people make the first message they send resemble this:.

" Hi, this is John from the club last evening. I just intended to claim Hi, which I truly appreciate meeting you ... blah blah.".

Don't do that! It's monotonous and also, even worse, it doesn't oblige her to respond.

Right here is an unfortunate fact that you need to understand ...

You Are Not Special To Her!

OK, perhaps I didn't need to shriek. Sorry regarding that.

However, pay attention, the fact is, the lady (especially if she's hot) most likely offered her numbers bent on several different men last evening (women do that.) Sending some vanilla text messages is not going to make her remember you. And also, if she does not recognize you, she won't respond!

Rather you should say something attention-grabbing that additionally associates with the time when you satisfied her. Something like ...

" Man, what was the deal with that insane guy on the dancing floor last night?! I think he gave me a shiner - John".

Or ...

" Oh my god. I simply realized who you resemble ...".

Ladies are VERY interested in their looks, and also this declaration is sure to pique her passion.

By bring up something amusing or intriguing that happened last night, you not just remind her that you yet likewise draw her back to the psychological state that she was in when she satisfied you (and having fun.) This is a very powerful strategy and also extremely important for building tourist attractions (a lot more on this in various other articles.).

Harmful Text Game Error # 3: Sending Texts That Are Too formal.

Remember, you are trying to talk to this woman, not audit her tax obligations. So do not send her messages like ...

" Dear Stacey, I'm pleased we had an opportunity to speak last evening, and I had a delightful time ...".

Instead, speak with her like you 2 are already friends. Be playful, teasing, and enjoyable. Don't be afraid to use jargon, misspellings, and unfinished sentences. If she is foreign or is highly informed and is turned by bad grammar and slang.), (The obvious exception would certainly be.

Male, I think I simply had the weirdest day of my life. Yours has to be quite insane, I wager.".

This message likewise offer to excite her inquisitiveness and make her wonder what was so strange about your day.

Remember, our supreme goal is to escalate the messages to this woman to a sex-related degree, so it's best to begin off with a lively tone instead of an official one.

Now you may be thinking that you'd never make these stupid errors, but I can not inform you the number of men I've seen repetitively make these text mistakes and destroy their chances to sleep with so many hot girls.

Don't make the same errors. The challenges that I've discussed could seem necessary but by avoiding them, you can increase or triple your chances with a girl.

Texting Women - What You Don't Know Can Hurt You

Hundreds and hundreds of ladies from throughout the globe have the same view when it comes to guys and their texting methods, they are clueless. We rant and also rave when one gets it right. If we have relocated onto another, we conserve their messages and carry them around on our phones too.

Guys, when texting, women are just doing communications at a minimum. They aren't engaging the female or her spirited nature. If you are sending anything similar to the following as texts, you may intend to proceed with analysis;

Greetings

Great Morning Sexy

Great Night

Hope you are having a good day

How is your day

Just how is such and also such

How are you today

Do not work to tough

What are you doing

I am doing such and such

Thinking about you

I enjoyed last evening

There is nothing in the above messages to engage a woman and build up her tourist attraction. It's just idle conversation. Unless a lady is smitten with a man, these messages will certainly simply make her eyes roll.

While you are sending her those lame messages, there might well be an individual who is shaking her globe with the best words and also techniques. It's the mysterious individual, the one that engages our creativity that presses our buttons.

Suzanne is a carefree, no-nonsense southerly woman. He opened the message with Scarlett, as in O'Hara. What woman would certainly not desire to be seen that way?

That individual recognized exactly how to engage her and also press her switches. She even knew he had paid interest to her. Talk about brushing a lady's ego.

When texting ladies, leave the little talk conversations out of it. If you can't flirt and be lively and make her smile, placed down the phone, or else you are merely tossing cold water on the fire. You intend to problem her to where when she sees it is you texting, she gets thrilled, and her heart avoids a beat. You intend to be the man that she saves his messages.

CHAPTER SIX

Texting Tips to Create Massive Attraction

Neglecting her, and having tons of fish on the line

A lot of men will concentrate only on one woman and at the very same time drive her away, why is this? Now picture you have ten poles in the water, one wiggle; however, you do not give it the same level of interest because two others are showing the rate of interest at the very same time. The more fish you have interested in regarding your lure, the more significant the opportunities you are going to capture one, not only because of a numbers video game yet just since you physically can't also pay much interest to just one.

The Art of Push and Pull

Press and pull I have listened to in the PUA world a few times; however, I have never listened to an excellent explanation as to why it works, and I have never heard it applied to how to text a woman. Allow me to discuss how to relocate this useful tool, so there is no question as to just how to text a girl, flawlessly. (Let me add something, just checked out another "expert's" suggestions on just how to message ladies.

Why you ought to be a pain in the A ** over text.

Being complicated is a killer device for creating attraction over text since it requires the other person to play by your guidelines and not theirs. A whole lot of individuals, when texting a girl, will take an extra natural duty, given that they believe that if she "likes" you, she will undoubtedly choose you. Being challenging and not bowing to the will of a female is compelling and incredibly appealing when texting a woman.

Safety and comfort after that sex.

Above, we chat a lot about pressing her, being demanding, neglecting her, and just elevating your value by not being traditional. At the very same time, it is unbelievably essential to communicate that you are a risk-free individual, that you get along, that you are respectable. That sex is not your top priority. Luckily, massage is a terrific area to do this; with text, you can craft your response rather the knee jerk you might vomit out face to face. Not producing safety and convenience is the primary reason she closes the sex gates on your advancements. If you do not understand precisely how to message a woman appropriately and you send her something that is mildly hostile or excessively sexual, you will undoubtedly set off her flight reaction. Do you recognize why females like gay guys? Because they get their male repair with zero sex-related danger. I am not asking you to be effeminate around women (yet it does not injure) just to comprehend that even the smallest sexual, physical danger sends out ladies running. Exactly how does this convert to texting girls? Straightforward, keep sex speak with a minimum, maintain anger covered up, and existing them the best guy you can. Now mix that with being push/pull, and also you have a guy ALL ladies will be dumb brought in to. (Note, the risk is a kind of sexual stress, but this is a limited rope of tourist attraction, one that can take a lengthy time to master).

Your goal is proficiency, not many strategies and regulations.

I teach a load of rules and methods for texting girls; however, I don't require them anymore. Since I understand the secret of connection balance, something that, if recognized, will introduce you success, not just with texting women but in all relationships.

Should You Text Her? The Rules to Texting Women That You Want to Date.

A great deal of males in today's day and age usually ask yourself whether they ought to message women during the earlier phases of dating. Well, have you merely interesting and attractive female that you want to discover even more regarding? Should you message her?

For starters, when it comes to texting ladies, it would undoubtedly be vital for you to message them back if they message you. Indeed, it would likewise be alright for you to initiate the messages. If you always start the texts, how can you discover out if she is interested in you in return?

You are wrong if you assume that ladies that regularly reply to your text messages are certainly interested in you. Women who let men seek them are typically the ones that will be great with a few days here and there but will not get into connections with any individual. This is simply exactly how females work.

Now, there are likewise a great deal of men around that will certainly text women and maintain texting them till they get a reply. This would not be a good technique. If you make a decision that the solution to "Should you text her?" is indeed, yet she does not respond to you, there is probably a reason behind it

- and the reason generally isn't because she didn't receive your texts.

See, even if a woman didn't get your text message, she needs to text you at some time still if she is interested in you, so be a client. Should you message her?

On that note, you should not come and try up with reasons simply to message a female, either. Do not overshare points or be the first to open up with a woman.

So, generally, if you need to know the answer to "Should you text her?", keep in mind that you ought to always so if she texts you. Besides that, just do so if you understand you are doing the right thing to drive her tourist attraction through the roofing system.

For all of you individuals that might have a suitable ability degree with dating women, you may locate on your own regularly getting a telephone number. You head out in the evening with your close friends, wind up meeting a woman at bench or club and have excellent communication, and then you trade contact number. You may be thrilled after this happens, as you may think you have every little thing secured with her. Well, you and lots of others are not even near sealing any kind of take care of her. This is where you require to recognize how to message the woman.

When I first began Getting right into dating, I found that every woman I texted practically never responded to me. This is where you need some excellent text game.

For the ladies that are seemingly intoxicated, you need to message them within minutes, even if you are both still in the club. The ideal attempt would be to duplicate a joke using the message that you both laughed around during your communication. Not all girls get incredibly intoxicated, so below are ideas to have a successful text the next day.

Off, do not listen to anyone that has said to wait a couple of days before texting a girl. You need to message a lady the next day so she can be reminded of the experience you both had. One typical error that guys make and I used to make was just texting monotonous stuff like "Hey," "What's up," and also generic lines like that.

To make straightforward, simply experience the funny interactions you had with each other so she can be reminded of your worth. Texting is direct, yet numerous guys wind up losing girls with boring and predictable messages. Make her laugh, and also extra significantly, make her bear in mind why she spoke to you and also the worth you bring to the table as a male.

Do you ever get a woman's phone number and also discover on your shed with what activity to take following?

Let's claim you only me a woman at the bar or cocktail lounge, and also you both clicked and traded telephone numbers. If you do not text her, you want to date this woman and also are frightened you may destroy your chances with her. You message something like ... "Hi, Nice conference you," or "Hey, what's up?".

A lot of people end up losing females they meet because of sending a weak text. Sending out a positive text that will get feedback is very easy! Comply with these actions, and you will be turning your telephone number into dates quickly.

Step 1: Text her something referring to something that occurred between the both of you. This can be a within joke you both had throughout the interaction, or perhaps a commonality. Let's claim during your conversation with the lady; you both learned that you dislike enjoying the news and seafood. You can message her something like, "Hey Jen, wonderful meeting you last night. Let's capture up and also watch the Channel 7 News at some point over some crawfish (smiley face)".

Since it is simply a fast example, yet you understand. It is funny, and also shows that you bear in mind something about her. That sure as hell is most likely to spike her feelings a lot more than an easy text claiming, "Hi there exactly how are you?".

Send her a message that will undoubtedly remind her why you both clicked and also why she enjoyed it with you. A word like the one above is going to advise her of the fantastic experience she had with you and also will certainly make her more likely to text you back.

Action 2: Don't wait as well long to message her! Lots of people make the mistake of waiting too many days to message a female. Text her something that will have her laughing, and don't also wait long!

Step 3: Don't message her excessive. There is absolutely nothing even worse than a clingy person sending out hopeless texts. This will merely lead to no responses. Do not fret if she does not respond after the very first time. Wait a day or 2, and attempt again. Just DON'T sound clingy and determined.

Hopefully, these easy ideas will assist you out in your dating life and reveal you just how to message a lady. By dealing with the straightforward and also usual errors guys are making via text message, you will certainly observe a whole lot even more success with the women you meet.

When Texting Females Comply With Text Rules to Keep Them Thinking About You!

Texting ladies is a terrific method to keep the lines of interaction open, yet there still is message etiquette to comply with to maintain them thinking about you.

You can text ladies, without being so direct by getting the phone, or two indirect by dispatching an email. Text messaging is a terrific method to allow a person to understand you are assuming about them, without stressing that you are disrupting their routine.

When it comes to establishing strategies with a female, it is much better text rules to offer her a call instead of sending her off a text. If you are somewhat interested in a lady, you need to be putting in even more initiative, not less. This indicates not counting on texting as the primary method of interaction.

Texting females works best once you have now established a connection. It's a wonderful way to be teasing, without beginning as well strong. For circumstances, if you had a wonderful very first day with a female, adhering to up with a text that night allows her to know that you had a good time. It assures her that you are interested in her, without making you look as well excited.

The reality that you're touching base with a female is what's important, instead than worrying excessively about what to claim. Ladies like to understand that an individual they're into is thinking of them. Text etiquette has to do with preserving the link, and not regarding building a relationship by message.

Much like with calling or emailing a female, you still don't desire to be sending off way too many texts. Even though texting is a less straight type of communication, you can again encounter as also interested. Maintain some balance by evaluating exactly how frequent her message actions are to you. If she does not react back right away, do not stress.

Texting enables you to be much less inhibited and say something that you would not feel comfortable saying personally, or on the phone. Select up the phone rather if you desire to have a lengthier or even more meaningful conversation with a woman. You will certainly find as a lot more honest.

Being real for text etiquette, constantly be courteous in your messages. Don't use texting as a way to be upset or impolite with a female that rejects you, since it's easy to do it when she can't see you or hear you.

If you feel that what you said did not come throughout precisely, clarify it with her on the phone. New texting can make it worst.

How to Seduce Women on Online Dating Sites - Three Quick Tips to Success

Many men utilize on-line dating solutions not just because it's practical, but additionally, that ladies who are now on-line are 'much easier' to strategy since they are more open to making new pals. Read on to discover three fast pointers you can make use of to be much more reliable at finding your companion online and attain fantastic outcomes quickly ...

Tip Idea 1: "Appear As A NewbieRookie.

Once in a while, edit your online account so that you look that you are 'new.' This will make you a lot more eye-catching - bear in mind that any kind of reasonably 'aged' profile will give the impression that you have been seeking a long, very long time (which is not eye-catching!). Place on some fresh photos which make you look excellent - females often tend to screen our potential partners based on appearances, bear in mind that.

Suggestion # 2: "Similarity Breeds Familiarity." We are all brought in to individuals who resemble us. For that reason, when you zoom right into the profile of somebody you like, take a look at her leisure activities and passions. After that, modify your profile ahead across as somewhat similar to her. This will provide you a boost and also she will feel (subconsciously) that she likes you.

Suggestion # 3: "Hypnosis/ Fractionation". When you get her to talk with you online, it will certainly be useful to use some hypnosis strategies and tricks to make her like you a lot more (and get her intend to go out with you).

This method, called fractionation, has been used by professionals on the internet seducers to make ladies fall in love with them promptly. All you need to do is to make her go through an emotional rollercoaster with your conversation messages - and also 'anchoring' her pleased states with you.

But before you use this strategy, you have to heed this warning.

Fractionation is taken into consideration as a 'dark art' technique, which is the basis of hypnosis-based seduction. Also, while questionable, it is understood to be among one of the most efficient tactics ever before developed by underground reductionists.

It is described in a step-by-step system in the Deadly Seduction Manuscript (http://www.DeadlySeduction.com).

These psychology tactics are very unconventional methods that are used by the secret elite in the seduction Neighborhood. Use it at your own risk. I directly vouch for the efficiency of these tactics, yet care should be taken as they can be outright dangerous in the hands of the unethical.

How to Approach Women? Essential Tips You Need to Know

Due to gender differences, guys usually wait to speak to women. There can be several reasons behind this, but without going into its information, we can say that it has to be gotten rid of, and men need to be educated just how to come close to ladies with confidence. In this short article, we will certainly discuss some vital ideas you need to recognize to find true love. In your daily life, we come across with particular scenarios when we require to connect with women for a variety of reasons. Sometimes we get closer to among them, but quickly because of improper strategy, we have to step back to keep a normal relationship going.

First off, to get the exposure, you need to boost your social circle. This can be done by meeting more people in daily procedures. When you certainly meet extra new individuals in your life, they will certainly last an impact, which aids in building fundamental assumptions towards life. If you have a trendy lady in your course and you intend to date her. The very best method is to ask her to aid you in homework for which you can straight ask for her contact number. Once your relationship expands, it will be simpler interacting over personal issues and chatting regarding likes and disapproval leading towards making long-term love association.

You can go online and start communicating with women over dating sites. It is very vital to create an online account to allow others to see what kind of person you are.

You can ask a specialist who understands about love connections and can direct you over this on exactly how to target ideal resource to locate a real love. Love is something that speeds up an individual's capacity to execute his work. When you are in love, every little thing looks stunning, and also you begin considering points favorably.

CONCLUSION

There's a large amount of nuance in texting. But eventually, it's all about simplicity. The more comfortable your text messages are actually, the better a response they receive. Indeed, there's a great benefit to keeping things simple but very effective. That's why you acquired this book!

I hope that you have learned a lot from the topics covered in this book, and you are indeed ready to try out all the suggestions and tips. Whether it is your very first text to a new girl who contacts you just got or a follow-up text with a girl you haven't talked with in a long while, this book is specially dedicated to your success. Try it with a variety of girls at the very least 5 to 10 phone numbers. The night-and-day distinction in responses you receive will amaze you in positive ways.

Very often in life, certain things occur for a reason, and it's feasible that the women that deny you are doing you a massive favor, likely saving you a whole lot of time, power, and money being spent on the wrong woman for you.

Dating is a result of series activities, so the more phone numbers you get, the additional strategy that you get at conversing and moving closer to women. Your confidence is attached to your continued success with dating the women you develop an interest in.

When working with rejection coming from women when trying to date them, you should definitely not let a stranger possess so much power over you.